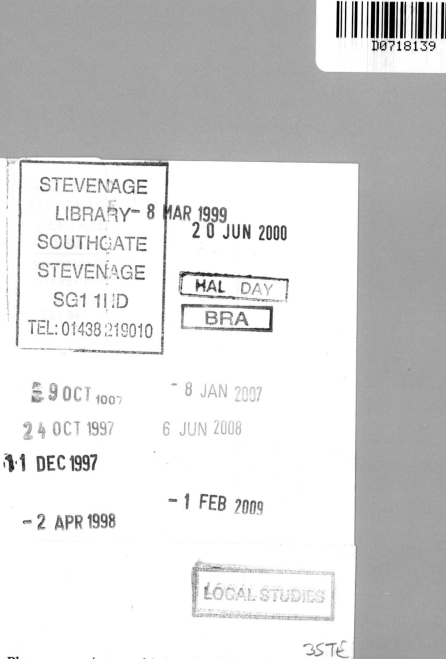

HERTFORDSHIRE'S
Queen

HERTFORDSHIRE'S
Queen

A CELEBRATION OF QUEEN ELIZABETH
THE QUEEN MOTHER'S
SPECIAL BOND WITH HER HOME COUNTY

Richard Whitmore

COUNTRYSIDE BOOKS
Newbury, Berkshire

First published 1997
© Richard Whitmore 1997

Countryside Books
3 Catherine Road
Newbury, Berkshire

ISBN 1 85306 491 2

*The photograph on page 2 shows The Queen Mother, with
Lady Bowes Lyon and Sir Martin Gilliat, walking
among the carnival floats during her 80th birthday
celebrations at St Paul's Walden, July 1980.*

Designed by Graham Whiteman
Produced through MRM Associates Ltd., Reading
Printed in Singapore

Contents

Introduction

'Old friends'

The late Reg Cannon, long-time editor of the *Hertfordshire Pictorial* and a respected mentor from my early years in journalism, used to tell a story about one Saturday afternoon in the 1920s when he was sent on a routine job to report a village fete at St Paul's Walden. Halfway having terrible trouble,' she said, 'Come and stand under here with me.'

Gratefully, Reg moved over to join the lass with the grey-blue eyes beneath her umbrella, which she insisted on holding over him and his notebook until the ceremony had finished. This friendly gesture was almost forgotten by the time Reg had

One photographer found a precarious perch to secure a picture of the royal car, carrying the new King and Queen, as it passed the Strathmore Arms in St Paul's Walden in 1937.

through the opening ceremony rain began to fall, soaking his notebook and making nonsense of his shorthand outlines. Spotting his predicament, a young woman standing nearby took pity. 'You seem to be cycled back to the office and typed up his report. Only years later, did it occur to him that he had another story to tell – about the day he shared an umbrella with the Queen of England!

Hertfordshire's Queen is an un-ashamedly home-spun book recalling Queen Elizabeth The Queen Mother's life-long bond with her English home county. A link that was forged with her birth in the summer of 1900 and progressed through her childhood days at St Paul's Walden Bury to the 1920s, when the dazzling Duchess of York set off on a world marathon of royal engagements that has lasted until the present day and is unlikely ever to be surpassed.

Since she left the Bury in 1923, not a year has passed when Queen Elizabeth hasn't returned. Her special affection for Hertfordshire and its people has never diminished. The Church; Medicine; New Towns; Education; Youth; The Army; Aviation; The Theatre; Horticulture – all have benefited from her patronage and her visits have highlighted many significant landmarks in the development of the county. So many visits, in fact, that it has proved quite impossible to include them all in this book.

However, any agonising over which events to include has been more than com-pensated by the pleasure of discovering again the treasure trove of photographs taken during a series of royal engagements that began three-quarters of a century ago. Such a collection could not have been assembled without the kindness of many local individuals and organisations, whose generosity is gratefully acknowledged on another page.

Most cameramen will tell you that it is quite difficult to take a bad picture of The Queen Mother, so adept is she at pro-viding each with a 'personal' shot. I first noticed this talent while standing beside a photographer colleague during Her Majesty's tour of Stevenage in 1956. As she walked back to the car, chatting with her escort, she seemed oblivious of us. Then, right on cue, her head turned and we found ourselves bathing in one of those lingering farewell smiles. Warm, yet bear-ing a hint of sadness that she had to be

A battery of box cameras
greets The Queen Mother
after she opened the High
School for Girls at Hitchin
in 1955. She is
accompanied by the
headmistress, Miss
Dorothy Gunn MBE.

'Before the rise of the paparazzi. Some 'old friends' from Hertfordshire newspapers awaiting The Queen Mother's arrival in 1959.

leaving so soon. With brilliant timing she had achieved direct eye contact in a fleeting second without even slowing her pace.

Very much aware of the problems cameramen face trying to keep ahead of their subject, Queen Elizabeth has been known to go to some lengths to help any who have missed a photo opportunity. At Bishop's Stortford College in 1968, Jim Lampin of the *Herts & Essex Observer* dashed into the college library for a shot of the royal guest signing the visitors' book, only to discover that she had already done it. 'Oh, dear! You're just too late!' she exclaimed. Then, sensing his disappointment, she added, 'Would you like a picture?' and promptly walked back to the table, picked up the pen and went through the motions of signing the book all over again. This empathy with the Press was demonstrated rather more forcefully another time, when Queen Elizabeth ticked off an over-zealous official who had tried to push a photographer out of her path. 'Please don't do that,' she said. 'Mr Devon and I are old friends – and we both have our work to do.'

A natural actress since early childhood (as the confident poses in those Edwardian photographs show) The Queen Mother's outstanding ability to temper regality with 'the common touch' has won her an ardent fan club among the traditionally hard-nosed representatives of the Fourth Estate. 'An intriguing mix of Queenship and the Sport of Kings,' as Donald Zec so neatly describes her in his royal biography. 'Part Gainsborough Lady, part Pearly Queen.' Qualities that pop up more than once in this affectionate record of Hertfordshire's proud link with the most enduring and much-loved member of our royal family. A Queen as old as the century whom most of us would vote 'Lady of the Century' as well.

Richard Whitmore
St Ippolyts, 1997

1900

The riddle on the birth certificate

'It cannot be explained, nor is it likely that it ever will.'

For much of this century the people of Hertfordshire thought they had the soundest possible reason to claim Queen Elizabeth The Queen Mother as 'their' queen. Namely, that Elizabeth Bowes Lyon, the commoner who became Queen Consort to King George VI and thereby India's last Empress, was actually born in the county at St Paul's Walden. There was no cause to think otherwise because it says so on her birth certificate and is further confirmed by the inscription on a stone plaque in the parish church; a plaque which King George watched her unveil a few months after their Coronation and which includes the words: '*Her Majesty Queen Elizabeth was born in this Parish Aug 4 1900. Baptised in this Church Sept 23 1900 and here worshipped.*'

Then, in May 1980, as she and we were preparing to celebrate that memorable 80th birthday, Queen Elizabeth suddenly declared that she was born not in Hertfordshire but in London. In doing so, she set in motion a debate that seems unlikely ever to be resolved.

It all began when a booklet and programmes produced by the St Paul's Walden community for the 80th birthday celebrations stated (on the advice of Clarence House) that Queen Elizabeth had 'spent her childhood years in the parish' – ignoring the far more significant fact that she had been born there. This inconsistency caught the eye of a local journalist who sent the story to the *Sunday Times.* Then, when a copy of Elizabeth's birth certificate was obtained from the superintendent registrar at Hitchin, it showed that her father Lord Glamis hadn't registered the birth until September 21, which was six days beyond the 42-day limit permitted by the Registration of Persons Act of 1837.

When the *Sunday Times* put these points to the Clarence House spokesman they were told that it could only be because Lord Glamis had not given the correct facts of the birth. The newspaper (presumably with tongue in cheek) noted that this amounted to a false registration which, under the Forgery Act of 1861, could have led to conviction as a felon and penal servitude for life. As it was, the kind and upright Lord Glamis had only to pay a nominal penalty of 7s 6d – for failing to register the birth of an infant within the required six week period.

So, if it wasn't Hertfordshire, where exactly in London was The Queen Mother born? Was Her Majesty aware of the error on the church tablet when she unveiled it back in 1937? The spokesman, now sounding slightly bemused by all this fuss, told the *Daily Telegraph*: 'I don't suppose she realised there was an inaccuracy. She

has always known she was born in London . . . Where The Queen Mother was born is really so unimportant.'

As for Lord Glamis giving the registrar incorrect details of his baby's arrival: 'It cannot be explained, nor is it likely that it ever will. The reason for this inaccuracy must be open to speculation.' Well, there has certainly been plenty of that in the ensuing years. A popular theory is that not long after Elizabeth's birth – with mother and child 'doing well' – Lord Glamis and the older children took the train north for the family's annual summer holiday on their Scottish estate at Glamis. Returning to the Bury in September, his lordship learned that the baby's christening was to take place on Sunday the 23rd. On Friday the 21st, realising that he hadn't yet registered Elizabeth's birth, he hurried into Hitchin, only to be told by Mr Baylis

the registrar that he had broken the law. In something of a fluster and with the christening imminent, he had given St Paul's Walden as the place of birth instead of the London address. That's the theory.

However, since this debate had its first public airing in 1980, a measure of evidence has emerged to indicate that, while Lord Glamis was tardy in registering the birth of his ninth and most famous child, he may have been right when he said she was born at St Paul's Walden. Perish the thought, but could it be that it is The Queen Mother who has been misinformed?

Much of this evidence was gleaned by the Rev Dendle French, then Vicar at All Saints, who had taken the brunt of the press inquiries and became intrigued by the mystery. He managed to trace a daugh-

THE ORGAN AND THIS TABLET WERE
PLACED IN THE CHURCH BY A PARISHIONER
TO THE GLORY OF GOD
AND IN MEMORY OF THE CORONATION OF
THEIR MAJESTIES KING GEORGE VI &
QUEEN ELIZABETH MAY 12TH 1937
HER MAJESTY QUEEN ELIZABETH
WAS BORN IN THIS PARISH AUGUST 4TH 1900
BAPTISED IN THIS CHURCH SEPT 23RD 1900
AND HERE WORSHIPPED

Parishioners studying the Coronation tablet in All Saints' church, St Paul's Walden, shortly after it had been unveiled by The Queen in November 1937. Although Her Majesty has since said she was born in London, not Hertfordshire, there are no plans to have it removed or altered.

ter of the Rev Tristan Valentine, who had conducted the baptism service. He found Miss Margaret Valentine, a sprightly 91 year old, living in a retirement home at Reading. She was 11 when Elizabeth Bowes Lyon was born and told Mr French that she vividly remembered being in the middle of piano practice when one of the family came running over to the Vicarage from the Bury with news that Lady Glamis had just given birth to a girl. She was absolutely sure the birth had taken place at St Paul's Walden.

Then Mr French received a letter from the family of the Welwyn doctor who, they said, attended the birth and was one of the local community invited to Lady Elizabeth's wedding in 1923. Although the writer had no concrete evidence that Lady Glamis' confinement had been at the Bury, it seemed highly unlikely that a doctor from a village in deepest Hertfordshire would be called to attend upon a birth in London.

Finally, there are the reports passed down by word of mouth through old parish families. Still heard today is a remark reputedly made by one of the women working in the Bury's laundry that August day in 1900. 'From the state of the bed linen, her ladyship must have had a difficult time with the birth.'

So there, for the record, are the two sides of a small but historically irritating discrepancy in The Queen Mother's life. What is undisputed is that the young Lady Elizabeth spent many happy years growing up in Hertfordshire and it was at her home in St Paul's Walden that she accepted the proposal of marriage that was to take her on her momentous journey through the rest of the 20th century.

Two Benjamins and Bobs . . .

An Edwardian childhood

Elizabeth Angela Marguerite Bowes Lyon was the ninth of ten children born to Lord and Lady Glamis, Scottish aristocrats whose family, with its Earldom of Strathmore, is descended from King Robert the Bruce. In 1372, Sir John Lyon was given Glamis Castle, a rather forbidding fortress 12 miles north of Dundee and reputed to be the oldest inhabited building in Britain. The Strathmores' English estates were acquired about 400 years later in 1767 when another John Lyon, the 9th Earl of Strathmore, married Mary-Eleanor Bowes. Her father George had died seven years earlier when she was only 11. With no brother to inherit the estate Mary-Eleanor became one of the wealthiest children in the country, as heiress to a castle and land in County Durham and – in Hertfordshire – St Paul's Walden Bury, the rambling red-brick Queen Anne house that sits so comfortably on rising farmland above the village of Whitwell. On his marriage to Mary-Eleanor, John Lyon was obliged by the terms of her father's will to adopt the additional name of Bowes, thus starting the Bowes Lyon family line. For a while they were known as Lyon-Bowes, until the 13th Earl (The Queen Mother's grandfather) decided to change the name around to its present form.

In 1904, as Elizabeth was approaching her fourth birthday, the 13th Earl died and her father Claude George succeeded him to become the 14th Earl of Strathmore and Kinghorne, Viscount Lyon and Baron Glamis, Tannadyce, Sidlaw and Strathdichtie in Scotland; Baron Bowes of Streatlam Castle in County Durham and Lunedale in County York. His estates, reflecting his extensive title, covered a total of 65,000 acres in Scotland, County Durham and Hertfordshire.

Elizabeth, who inherited the courtesy title of Lady upon her grandfather's death, was separated from her five older brothers and two sisters by seven years. The Strathmores' first daughter, Violet, had died in 1893 at the age of 11. With the older siblings away at school, Lady Elizabeth became closely attached to her baby brother David, who arrived in 1902. Their mother dubbed the pair – her ninth and tenth children – 'my two Benjamins', after the two smallest of our ten toes.

The Countess of Strathmore, formerly Cecilia Cavendish-Bentinck was the

A rare picture of the entire Strathmore family at the Bury c1905. Standing (l to r) are Fergus (later killed in action in 1915), John, the Earl, Mary, the oldest son Patrick, and Alexander (who died in 1911 aged 24). In the front row are Rose, the Countess (with a wriggling David on her knee), Elizabeth and Michael. The oldest daughter, Violet, had died in 1893 at the age of 11.

They could also be a bit of a handful, though Elizabeth's childhood vices appear to have been few. Once, when she was six, she found a pair of scissors and cut a set of brand new bed sheets into strips. When discovered she confessed and escaped with a maternal reprimand. On another occasion, according to a story handed down through estate families, the Earl discov-

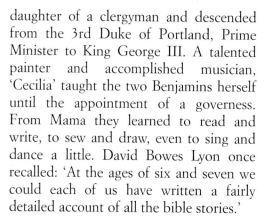

Elizabeth and her brother David on the Bury terrace, wearing their garden smocks. The Queen Mother once recalled that their unsmiling faces were the result of heated debate over who was to hold the wheelbarrow.

daughter of a clergyman and descended from the 3rd Duke of Portland, Prime Minister to King George III. A talented painter and accomplished musician, 'Cecilia' taught the two Benjamins herself until the appointment of a governess. From Mama they learned to read and write, to sew and draw, even to sing and dance a little. David Bowes Lyon once recalled: 'At the ages of six and seven we could each of us have written a fairly detailed account of all the bible stories.'

ered little footprints and evidence of scrumping in the Bury's carefully-tended fruit gardens. He summoned his head gardener and asked who had done it.

'The children, I'm afraid my lord,' replied the gardener diplomatically.

'I know that,' said his lordship. 'But whose, man? Yours or mine?'

'Yours, I'm afraid my lord.'

'Well, next time you catch them,' said his lordship, 'you have my permission to put your hand across them.'

In the loft of a ruined brewhouse the two youngsters had a secret den which they had christened 'The Flea House'. Here they hoarded such illicit luxuries as sweets, bars of chocolate – and once, it's recorded, a supply of Woodbine cigarettes and

An early view of the Bury, showing its generous covering of honeysuckle and magnolia.

Lady Elizabeth and 'Bobs' on the Bury lawns in 1909.

matches! Here was where they scampered to hide when playing truant from lessons. It wasn't always easy for the grown-ups to retrieve them because the rickety state of the loft ladder made it unsafe for anyone heavier than a child to climb.

The young woman most often called upon to sort out this mischief was Clara Cooper Knight, daughter of a local farmer, who joined the Strathmore family as nurse-maid at the age of 17, not long after Elizabeth's birth. Nicknamed 'Alah' from the early days when the two toddlers had trouble pronouncing her name, Clara devoted the rest of her life to the Strathmore family, eventually becoming royal nanny to the princesses Elizabeth and Margaret Rose. In her later years, she was known as Mrs Knight, even though she never married.

Throughout each year the Strathmores moved regularly between their three homes. A short season in London at the Earl's recently-acquired Adam house in St James's Square would precede a long summer holiday in Scotland at Glamis, followed by winter in Hertfordshire at the Bury. Each October, after they had arrived and settled in, the butler would announce to the assembled staff: 'His Lordship will be here now until the sap rises.' Meaning February or March, depending on the severity of the winter.

Christmas was celebrated at the Bury until the outbreak of the First World War. With Glamis Castle converted into a military hospital, the teenage Lady Elizabeth went to Scotland with the Countess to spend the duration helping to care for wounded servicemen. It was there, in 1915, that she learned that her brother Fergus, a captain with the Black Watch, had been killed in France at the battle of Loos.

Of the Strathmores' three contrasting homes, the Bury was undoubtedly the most suitable for two little Benjamins to spend their idyllic Edwardian childhood. Set in wonderful lakeside gardens full of walks, bowers and moss-covered statues it had none of the grand formality of a house in St James's Square or the sinister gloom of medieval Glamis Castle.

In Lady Elizabeth's young days the Bury fairly tumbled with animals as well as children. Dogs were everywhere. Chickens, too, including lots of pretty bantams 'whose eggs for tea are so good', she once told a friend. Then, Lucifer and Emma, the black Berkshire pigs, goats, rabbits and a tortoise. There was even a wild bullfinch named Bobby whose audacious habit of pinching crumbs from the nursery table led to his undoing when the cat got him. Brother David had to 'donate' his cedarwood pencil box to provide a coffin for the woodland burial ceremony, in which Bobby was seen safely off with special prayers led by our future Queen Mother.

However, of all the much-loved pets in Lady Elizabeth's personal animal kingdom none surpassed Bobs. He was a Shetland pony. Mane over eyes, straight from the Thelwell mould, he so adored his mistress that – given the opportunity – he would fol-

low her everywhere. Round the garden, up and down stone steps; sometimes even into the house. It is Bobs whose memory is perpetuated in the lovely photograph taken at the Bury when Lady Elizabeth was nine and showing her riding side-saddle in the confident pose of an accomplished Edwardian horsewoman. Behind her can be seen the clipped yew hedges leading to the woodland walks where, one Sunday in 1923, history would be made.

Like many mothers, the Countess of Strathmore used the services of local photographers to record her growing family. This picture of Lady Elizabeth was taken in the studios of Frederick Thurston at Luton.

1923

'A woodland wooing'

According to certain socialites of the period Bertie, otherwise HRH Prince Albert, Duke of York, first set his sights on Elizabeth Bowes Lyon in 1920 when he saw her dancing with his equerry at the Royal Air Force Ball in London. Over the next two years, as their friendship blossomed, The Duke paid a number of short visits to both the Bury and Glamis Castle, from where he once wrote to his mother Queen Mary: 'It is delightful here & Elizabeth is very kind to me. The more I see of her the more I like her.'

Although it had become clear in Court circles that he was very much in love, some were less sure that Lady Elizabeth would marry him. They felt she had doubts about exchanging her pleasant close-knit family life for the exposure and scrutiny that would come with being the daughter-in-law of the monarch. Her father the Earl's opinion of royalty had also dipped somewhat after learning of the vigorous extra-marital activities of Bertie's grandfather, King Edward VII.

Consequently, Bertie is believed to have had to make at least two proposals of marriage before he was finally accepted. After the first, Elizabeth's mother had told a friend: 'I like him so much and he is a man who will be made or marred by his wife.' King George and Queen Mary had also fallen under Elizabeth's spell and were very keen for their quiet and stammering second son to make the match.

So, on Saturday 13th January 1923, The Duke left his anxious parents waiting at York Cottage, Sandringham and set off for St Paul's Walden on another mission to secure the hand of Elizabeth Bowes Lyon. 'You'll be a lucky feller if she accepts you,' The King had told him.

On Sunday morning, while the rest of the family were at church, Lady Elizabeth and The Duke left the Bury for a winter walk through the woodland glades where she had spent so much of her idyllic childhood. It was there that Bertie chose to put the question for the third time – and was accepted. Back at the Bury later that day, The Duke went with the Earl into the morning room to formally ask for Elizabeth's hand. It was given, of course, but while the Earl rejoined Elizabeth and the rest of the family to begin their celebrations, The Duke had one more job to do. Picking up the telephone he sent a prearranged coded telegram to his parents at Sandringham. It consisted of three words: 'All right, Bertie.'

On Monday, the Court Circular announced: 'It is with great pleasure that The King and Queen announce the betrothal of their beloved son The Duke of York to Lady Elizabeth Bowes Lyon, daughter of the Earl and Countess of Strathmore, to which The King has gladly given his consent.'

Hard on the heels of the announcement, a reporter from the *Herts Mercury* went to the Bury and obtained an interview with the Earl, who was discovered gardening in the grounds 'armed with a pruning hook'. His lordship told the newspaper that the couple had first met at a children's party when Lady Elizabeth was aged about five or six – the party, no

(opposite) The Bride-Lady Elizabeth Bowes Lyon: a portrait by John St Helier Lander in 1923.

(The Illustated London News Picture library)

[Printed by authority of the Registrar General.]

CERTIFIED COPY of an
Pursuant to the Births and

Registration District	Hitchin and

1900 Birth in the Sub-district of _Hitchin_

Columns:— 1	2	3	4	5
No. When and where born	Name, if any	Sex	Name, and surname of father	Name, surname and maiden surname of mother
269 Fourth August 1900 St Paul's Walden Bury. Saint Pauls walden RD.	Elizabeth Angela Marguerite	Girl	Claude George Bowes Lyon.	Cecilia Nina Bowes Lyon. Formerly Cavendish Bentinck

Certified to be a true copy of an entry in a register in my

CAUTION:—It is an offence to falsify a certificate or to make or knowingly use a false certificate or a copy of a false certificate intending it to be accepted as genuine to the prejudice of any person, or to possess a certificate knowing it to be false without lawful authority.

WARNING: THIS CERTIFICATE IS NOT EVIDENCE OF THE IDENTITY OF THE PERSON PRESENTING IT.

RY OF BIRTH

ths Registration Act 1953

age .

the   *County of Hertford .*

	7	8	9	10*
father	Signature, description, and residence of informant	When registered	Signature of registrar	Name entered after registration
	Glamis Father St Pauls Walden Bury Saint Pauls walton	Twenty first September 1900	C H Baylis Registrar.	

*See note overleaf.

M Bird   Superintendent Registrar

24th September 1996 Date

(opposite) *A happy bridegroom and bride on their wedding day, 26 April 1923*

(The Illustrated London News Picture library)

How the 'Herts Mercury' broke the news of the royal engagement.

Y. SATURDAY, JANUARY 20, 1923.

THE ROYAL LOVE ROMANCE.

WOODLAND WOOING IN HERTFORDSHIRE.

LADY BOWES-LYON WELL KNOWN IN THE COUNTY.

The welcome news of the Duke of York's betrothal to Lady Elizabeth Bowes-Lyon, the youngest daughter of the Earl of Strathmore, of St. Paul's Walden Bury, near Hitchin, and of Glamis Castle,-For-

Walden Bury on Sunday after tea.

The prospective union is not the first which the house of Strathmore has made with a Royal family. It is recalled that

[Photo Claude Harris, Ltd., Regent Street.

Lady Elizabeth Bowes-Lyon.

The Bride-to-be.

[By Photopress, London.

The Duke of York.

A New and Unpublished Photograph.

farshire, has given unqualified satisfaction to all sections of the community.

To Hertfordshire it is particularly pleasing, as the happy young Royal bride-to-be has spent the greater part of her life in her father's Hertfordshire home. She is most popular with all the tenants and employees on the estate and the

Sir John Lyon, an ancestor of Lady Elizabeth, who was Chamberlain of Scotland in 1377, married Jean, daughter of King Robert II.

Lady Elizabeth Bowes-Lyon is not only very fond of dancing, but has the reputation of being one of the best dancers in society.

She is credited with being extremely

[By Photopress, London.

WHERE THE WOOING TOOK PLACE.

*Elizabeth aged 15,
fingering a necklace.*

ment did not take us altogether by surprise, as the friendship has ripened since The Prince was our guest at Glamis Castle.'

The widespread pleasure felt by Hertfordshire people was summed up by the *Mercury* under its headline: 'Woodland Wooing in Hertfordshire'! 'To Hertfordshire it is particularly pleasing, as the happy young Royal bride-to-be has spent the greater part of her life in her father's Hertfordshire home. She is most popular with all the tenants and employees on the estate and the villagers of Whitwell, which is only half-a-mile away. They have known her ever since she first came to St Paul's Walden Bury as a baby less than 12 months old. Her Ladyship in turn knows everyone in the village by name and always has a kind word for anyone she meets in her strolls round the estate. . . .

'Lady Elizabeth is not only very fond of dancing but has the reputation of being one of the best dancers in society. She is credited with being extremely musical and is gifted with a considerable amount of tact which, together with her social experience gained at the right hand of her mother in a great house, will of course be immensely valuable to her when, as Duchess of York, she takes her place amongst the great British hostesses.'

The newspaper's prediction that the engagement would be 'comparatively short' was correct. Bertie and Elizabeth were married at Westminster Abbey just over three months later, on 26th April. While waiting to begin their walk down the aisle, the bride and her father found themselves standing beside the Tomb of the Unknown Warrior. On a sudden impulse, Elizabeth stooped down and placed her bouquet of white York roses and Scottish heather at its head. It was one of those timely, spontaneous gestures for which the newest member of the Royal Family was to become famous.

doubt, at which she is said to have given Bertie the cherries from the top of her piece of cake. 'They have been friendly ever since and have met frequently in town and country,' the Earl said. 'The engage-

1924-1936

'The smiling Duchess'

Although nobody could have known it at the time, Elizabeth Bowes Lyon's woodland betrothal on that January day in 1923 was to take us into the second Elizabethan Age. An appropriate historical coincidence when one remembers that the first one also began in a Hertfordshire wood just a few miles from St Paul's Walden. On a similar winter's day in 1558 Princess Elizabeth was sitting beneath an oak tree in the park of Hatfield Palace when courtiers came to tell her of her accession to the Tudor throne.

The present Hatfield House, built in Jacobean days alongside the Old Palace,

has been visited by Queen Elizabeth The Queen Mother probably more times than even she can remember. Through her great friendship with three generations of the Cecil family, in particular 'Bobbety and Betty' (Robert, the 5th Marquess of Salisbury and his wife Elizabeth), she has been a regular guest at Hatfield since childhood. It was there, too, that she made her first public appearance in Hertfordshire as a member of the Royal Family.

In May 1924 more than 14,000 people poured into Hatfield Park to see 'the smiling Duchess' as Fleet Street had affectionately christened her. The occasion was

'The Smiling Duchess' - the image remembered when Lady Elizabeth returned to the county a member of the Royal Family.

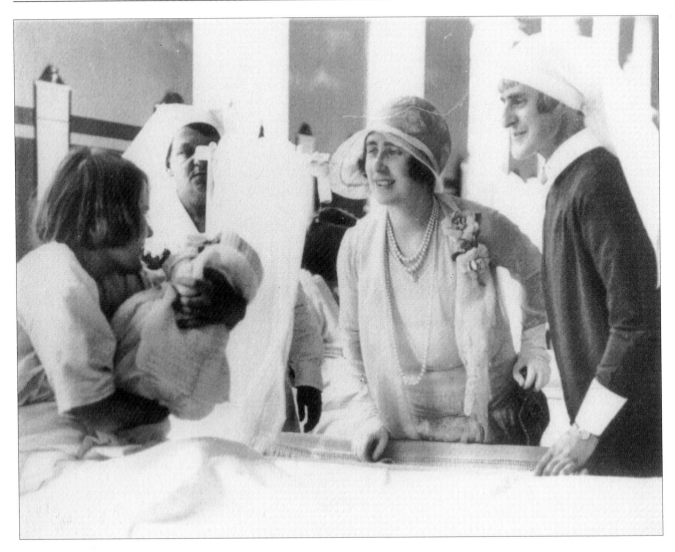

Admiring the latest arrival in the maternity ward of North Herts Hospital, Hitchin in July 1929, with the matron Miss F.K. Bell.

an Elizabethan Fete organised by Alice, Marchioness of Salisbury in aid of the county's nursing organisations. With post-war Britain in recession and no Welfare State to bring relief to the millions of poor, the demands made on voluntary organisations were heavy. Competition for royal patronage to enhance fund-raising projects became intense and – as the enchanting new member of King George V's rather staid family – none was more in demand than The Duchess of York.

In Hertfordshire, as across the country, she gave special support to projects aimed at improving hospital facilities. In 1929 she was at Hitchin, in 1933 Bishop's Stortford and a year later at Welwyn village, to open new hospital wings, or in

the case of Welwyn a complete cottage hospital, built with money bequeathed by a millionaire resident, Sir Otto Beit. Of course, with millionaire benefactors thin on the ground, most campaigns had to be financed by a local appeal and as these touched on just about every organisation in the community, the number of guests at opening ceremonies could sometimes be overwhelming.

When The Duchess came to Hitchin to open a new wing of the North Herts and South Beds Hospital in Bedford Road (where a supermarket now stands) there were almost 1,000 names on the guest list – far too many to squeeze into the hospital grounds. So a 'long-distance' opening ceremony was devised half a mile away on the lawns of Hitchin Priory. There, instead of cutting a tape, the royal guest was invited to set off a siren that sounded across the town, providing the cue for a flag to be hoisted over the hospital.

At Hitchin, as at Welwyn and Bishop's Stortford, the event included a rather pretentious ceremony that had become an almost obligatory feature of royal charity visits during those years, when long lines of cute little girls and well-groomed little boys were marshalled onto the dais, each to present Her Royal Highness with a velvet purse containing the money raised by a particular group.

After receiving 30 or 40 of these; after numerous handshakes, the presentation of long-service medals, and then several lengthy and eloquent tributes, The Duchess always kept her own speech to a minimum. At Bishop's Stortford and Welwyn she spoke for little more than 30

seconds, while the 1,000 expectant guests at Hitchin heard her utter just nine words: 'I have much pleasure in declaring this wing open.' Our future Queen Mother had already decided that time was better spent meeting people rather than addressing them.

Touring the Hitchin hospital later that afternoon The Duchess revealed her talent for recognising faces and names from the past. In one ward she spotted the bed-ridden figure of Jim Parsons, a retired blacksmith from St Paul's Walden. Progress was delayed a few moments while they reminisced about Elizabeth's childhood visits to his forge to watch the Earl's horses being shoed.

Unlike the rest of the royal family at this time, the young Duchess approached each event as though it was a fresh experience. *The Times* newspaper noted: 'She lays a foundation stone as though she has

'Purse children' offering a variety of bows and curtsies at the opening of the Queen Victoria Memorial Hospital, Welwyn, July 1934.

just discovered a new and delightful way of spending an afternoon.' It is a skill that has remained with her throughout public life and one which does wonders for nervous organisers. Coupled with this has been her instinctive ability to communicate with people of all classes – something the regal training of that period had yet to achieve.

Until the work of an up-and-coming fashion designer named Norman Hartnell caught her eye in 1937, The Duchess of York had been content to follow fashion rather than set it – relying on the creations of Queen Mary's dressmaker, Madame Handley Seymour, who had made her wedding gown. Nevertheless, every outfit was scrutinised closely by the fashion writers of the day. At Welwyn, 'Her Royal Highness looked enchanting in an exquisite shade of misty blue – rather like Love-in-a-Mist – with ropes of pearls and a most becoming hat with a wreath of tiny flowers cunningly passed under the hair at the back.' At Hitchin she 'looked charming in an ensemble of pale pink. Her crinoline and lace hat was in her usual style with a broad brim dipping at the sides. Her dress was of chiffon and lace with an uneven hem. She wore round her neck a treble rope of pearls and carried a black and white parasol and a raffia pochette.'

However, fashion epithets were harder to find when The Duchess came to Hatfield again in June 1931. Invited to review some 4,000 of the county's Girl Guides she appeared in the formidable dark serge uniform of a Guide Commissioner, complete with wide-brimmed hat, gauntlet gloves, lanyard and whistle. 'Looking neat' was the best anyone could come up with on that occasion.

In fact, Lady Elizabeth had worn uniforms from time to time since becoming district commissioner of the Glamis and Eassie Girl Guides in 1921 and later Commandant-in-Chief of the St John Nursing Divisions. However, the photograph at Hatfield was one of the last taken before she made up her mind never to wear uniforms again. It was a decision she stood by even during the war years when she was Commandant-in-Chief of all three women's services. The reason was quite simple. She felt she no longer had the figure for them. 'Some clothes,' she said, 'just do not like me.'

1929-1979

'Visiting dear Hitchin'

There's an impressive mahogany mantelpiece in a certain Hitchin home upon which – the owners will tell you – Queen Elizabeth The Queen Mother once sat. They then explain to the bewildered visitor that the mantelpiece in question was made from a large counter that once stood in their family's hardware store and upon which three year old Elizabeth Bowes Lyon was frequently parked while her nursemaid was ordering goods.

There are probably more 'Queen Mum' stories in Hitchin than in any other town in the county because, since that day in 1900 when the town's registrar issued her birth certificate, Hitchin has had a rather special association with The Queen Mother. Sitting neatly in a tree-ringed hollow below a ridge of the Chiltern Hills, this medieval market town is less than five miles from St Paul's Walden; an easy journey for the pony and trap in which Elizabeth made her first shopping expeditions and which later took her to school there.

Her tutor, Marion Wilkie, was one of several governesses who taught the four youngest Strathmore children – Rose, Michael, Elizabeth and David – during the years between 1904 and 1913. She travelled regularly to the Bury to give morning lessons before lunching with the family and returning home to Hitchin. 'High-spirited and mischievous,' was how she once described her charges. 'Their favourite game was to entice me for a walk in the woods and detain me there so that there would be no time to go over their studies!'

Following an illness, Miss Wilkie found the daily journey to the Bury too tiring and it was then that the Countess allowed the two Benjamins to travel into Hitchin to Miss Wilkie's house, 'Lopside', in Dacre Road. There, with two other youngsters – Guy Gainsford, son of a local vicar, and Dorothy Harris – Elizabeth and David continued their education almost until the war, when David went off to preparatory school and Elizabeth to Glamis Castle with her mother.

Interviewed in July 1929, when her former pupil returned to Hitchin as The Duchess of York, Miss Wilkie said her most abiding memory of young Elizabeth was the 'pretty sight' of her on her pony, wearing a dashing riding habit of bright scarlet. That and her natural talent for dancing, for which she and David took lessons each week in the ballroom of Hitchin's historic coaching inn, the Sun Hotel.

So perhaps it is hardly surprising that the town has a special place in The Queen Mother's heart, preserving as it does memories of what were probably the happiest years of her life: her carefree childhood and the comfortable post-war period of the 1920s and early 1930s, when she and The Duke of York were as close as they ever could be to living the life of 'an ordinary family'. They could drive into town with the children to browse round their favourite shops, still unaware that the family would one day have to shoulder the awesome burdens of monarchy.

Whenever she has come to Hitchin, Queen Elizabeth has reminded its people of her affection for the town – as in 1955

when she came to open a new school: 'It is always a great happiness to me to come back to Hertfordshire, especially to Hitchin, whose lovely old streets and market square hold many happy memories for me,' she said.

One of those memories must be of William Upchurch's antiques gallery in Bancroft, premises now occupied by a burger restaurant. The Upchurchs had served the Strathmore family since the end of the 19th century and the shop became a favourite port of call for The Duke and Lady Elizabeth. Tea was always provided in a special bone china service whenever they arrived to peruse the stock of antiques.

Three generations in a family photograph taken by Rachel Bowes Lyon in 1931. Princess Elizabeth and her mother have been using the pile of sand on the garden path to make a sandcastle. With them are David Bowes Lyon and the Countess of Strathmore.

Business was particularly brisk at the time of the royal wedding. First, Lady Elizabeth and her mother called in to buy a large lacquer cabinet for the Yorks' first home, White Lodge, in Richmond Park. Then Mr Upchurch supplied an inlaid mahogany card table, a wedding gift from tenant farmers on the Strathmore estate, after which came his own present, an inlaid satinwood lace box in which The Duchess later kept the lace wedding train given by Queen Mary. Mr Upchurch was the only Hitchin trader to be invited to Buckingham Palace for a private viewing of the astonishing 'Aladdin's Cave' of wedding gifts that had arrived from all over the

*To the delight of the crowd
The Queen Mother sets off
in July 1979 on an
unscheduled walk along
some of Hitchin's 'lovely old
streets' after a Service of
Thanksgiving in St Mary's
parish church.*

world. Even there, Lady Elizabeth spotted him among the large crowd and went over for a chat.

Just across the street from the Sun Hotel was Paternoster and Hales Ltd, newsagents, stationers and printers. Here was where Elizabeth and David were taken to stock up with pencils, crayons and exercise books for lessons. Later, during their teenage years, brother and sister would sometimes cycle to the shop from St Paul's Walden to pick up the Earl's newspapers.

By the 1930s, Paternosters' staff found themselves welcoming a new generation of royal customers. Mrs Valerie Dougherty remembers stopping to watch The Duchess of York's children, Lilibet and Margaret Rose, go into the shop with their grandmother Queen Mary – and

being consumed with schoolgirl envy as the nine year old future Queen Elizabeth II emerged carrying a copy of the latest *Mickey Mouse Annual*.

In July 1979, 50 years to the month after her first royal visit to the town, The Queen Mother came to a Service of Thanksgiving at St Mary's parish church, to celebrate the completion of a preservation appeal. Afterwards, she was due to be driven to the Priory for a reception but, as she came out of church, she ignored her waiting limousine. Turning to her sister-in-law Lady Bowes Lyon she said: 'I think I will walk for a while.'

Then, to the consternation of her security men, she promptly set off towards the Priory on foot. One likes to think that, this time, her walkabout was not entirely for the benefit of the crowd. For, as Queen Elizabeth approached her 80th year, here was a rare chance to walk just once more along some of those 'lovely old streets' of her childhood. Past the oak-beamed shops in the Churchyard and across the ancient Market Place to Sun Street and the Sun Hotel where the two Benjamins had their dancing lessons. Past the red-brick building once occupied by Paternoster and Hales, purveyors of magical childhood goods, long gone, alas, but still commemorated by the bold embossed sign 'Printing Office' on the old facade high above the street.

Since that walkabout The Queen Mother's only other visit has been to give her name to Hitchin's new theatre but, as at least one resident will bear out, her lifelong love for the old town remains undiminished. Mrs Jean Anderson, a local president of Queen Mary's Clothing Guild, has met The Queen Mother quite regularly at guild gatherings in St James's Palace and was a guest at her 90th birthday celebrations. Whenever they meet, the royal patron's opening question is almost always the same:

'Now tell me first of all. How is *dear* Hitchin?'

The Duchess of York at Hitchin Priory, with Viscount Hampden, Lord Lieutenant of Hertfordshire. 1929.

'Coming home a Queen'

Although he is now remembered as one of our finest monarchs, George VI had neither expected nor wanted to be King; and it is a well-known fact that the calamitous events that brought about his accession are never discussed by The Queen Mother. Indeed, there is only one occasion when the abdication has been mentioned publicly by the Hertfordshire branch of her family – and then very briefly. During Queen Elizabeth's 80th birthday celebrations her sister-in-law, Lady Bowes Lyon, told a local newspaper of 'the great distress' she remembered at St Paul's Walden Bury on the December evening in 1936 when they heard Edward VIII's radio broadcast renouncing the throne for his love of the American divorcee Mrs Wallis Simpson.

'It was a great distress because of the events that occasioned it,' Lady Bowes Lyon said, adding that even her own family had never ventured to discuss it with The Queen when she came to Hertfordshire during the crisis. 'There was always a rigid code about what one did talk about and what was confidential,' she said. 'This was one of the confidential things – but from the beginning I was sure Queen Elizabeth was going to cope with it.' Others now go further, believing that The Queen Consort's love and firm support for her unhappy hus-

The Coronation of 1937 was given full coverage in the county's newspapers.

THEIR MAJESTIES THE KING AND QUEEN

LONG MAY THEY REIGN

band during that period saved a tottering monarchy from complete collapse.

Lady Bowes Lyon – formerly Rachel Spender Clay – had known The Duke and Duchess of York since the 1920s. She and David Bowes Lyon were married in 1929 and moved to the Bury two years later. Lady Bowes Lyon was to live there for more than 60 years until her death in 1996. The first time that she entertained her in-laws as King and Queen was in November 1937, when Queen Elizabeth unveiled the

very quiet one and the congregation will be limited to the usual worshippers resident in the village. Admission to the service will be by ticket only.'

The announcement seemed to be setting the tone for future visits to the Bury – a clear hint that the Royal Family wished to be allowed a short respite from formal duties among the informal pleasures of country life. They couldn't escape completely of course – not in Coronation Year – and that Sunday morning saw the narrow

The King planting a commemorative oak tree at St Paul's Walden under the critical eye of five year old Simon Bowes Lyon - who had just been restrained from doing the job himself.

Coronation plaque in All Saints' church. Along with an electric organ, the plaque had been donated by a churchwarden, the former MP for Hitchin, Major Guy Kindersley. The engraving on it was by his son David.

The royal visit was deliberately low-key. As a Court paragraph in *The Times* put it: 'The King and Queen will attend morning service tomorrow at the parish church of St Paul's Walden, near Hitchin, where the Queen will unveil a stone tablet to commemorate the fact that she was born in the parish and baptized in the church. Their Majesties wish the service to be a

country lane between the Bury and the church lined with people anxious for their first glimpse of Hertfordshire's Queen on her home patch.

In the afternoon, interest switched to the Bury grounds when estate families and children from Whitwell village school were invited to watch The King and Queen plant a pair of commemorative oak trees. It was during this ceremony that The Queen's five year old nephew Simon Bowes Lyon caused some hilarity when he briefly upstaged the monarch. Having watched his aunt place her token spadeful of soil on the roots of one tree

and concerned that she hadn't finished the job, he interrupted The King's part in the ceremony by picking up the spade and trying to shovel the rest of the earth into the hole himself.

Although young Simon's cousins, Lilibet and Margaret Rose, had remained at Windsor that weekend the royal children visited the Bury regularly throughout the 1930s. They were there for a while in 1939, when The King and Queen were away on a tour of Canada and the USA and had an unexpected surprise one evening when the butler came in to ask if they would care to take a transatlantic telephone call from their parents.

Lady Bowes Lyon remembered Princess Elizabeth as a child who enjoyed

A pair of Kings. King George VI 'off duty' and accompanied by Bert King, gamekeeper at St Paul's Walden.

life to the full. 'She was quick-witted and great fun because it was a fun family,' she said. 'She liked the general running about here and the feeling that it was her mother's home.' And, just as Mother had done in her childhood, the two princesses took their ponies through Reynolds Wood on mounted treasure hunts and enjoyed madcap sessions of charades in the evenings.

On the Saturday of their 1937 visit, King George spent the day shooting as he had done on most visits since the 1920s. Reg Smith of Hitchin remembers the pride he felt as a village lad when chosen to carry the shooting sticks and spare cartridge bags for the royal party. He still has vivid memories of watching the King's gun-dog retrieve a winged pheasant that had managed to glide to cover more than half a mile away. 'Young Smith', as the monarch called him, also did rather well financially. 'At the end of the day The King would pay me half a crown,' Reg tells you with a wink. 'Then, if I was quick, I could nip over and join the line of lads who'd been beating

and get another two bob from the head keeper!'

After an austere childhood as George V's brow-beaten second son, The King found the warmth of family life at the Bury a great tonic. 'His marriage and subsequent fatherhood was a wonderful thing for him,' said Lady Bowes Lyon, 'because it brought with it his first experience of a real home life.'

There is no more homely example of life at the big house than that found in the hallway just inside the garden door, where the height marks of several generations of Bowes Lyon offspring are recorded on the wall. The Queen Mother's name first appears in 1905, written by an adult but, an inch or two higher, in childish hand, is 'Elizabeth, December 1906'. There is also a rising series of marks for 'Lilibet' culminating with 'The Queen, July 1952' – a mark surprisingly low on the wall which leads one to assume that Her Majesty took off her shoes before being measured. Unlike her eldest son, who is recorded: 'Charles in shoes 1964.'

1940-42

'Somewhere in the Home Counties'

*I*n the pitch darkness of a wartime blackout, the royal train rumbled quietly into the sidings at Hitchin station. Protected by a cutting in the chalk hills, the spot offered ideal cover for an overnight stop as The King and Queen rested during their morale-boosting Battle of Britain tour. The secrecy surrounding their movements meant that only essential workers knew of the train's arrival, so very few were there to see King George and Queen Elizabeth climb down from their carriage and stretch their legs with a ten-minute stroll along the track before retiring for the night.

The royal couple played a vital role in lifting the spirits of the British people during those grim years. Because the country needed to see that the monarchy was alive and fighting fit, The King and Queen embarked on a series of tours up, down and across the country, covering an estimated half a million miles. They visited munitions factories, fire stations, barrage balloon sites and anti-aircraft gun units. They risked death from unexploded bombs as they toured blitzed communities to console the injured, the homeless and the bereaved.

With a telephone link to London to keep The King in constant touch with news from the war fronts, the royal train proved an ideal office-cum-home that enabled the couple to get on with the job in hand without too much interruption. For this reason, they quite often chose to spend the night in some remote railway siding sooner than accept an invitation to stay with the Lord Lieutenant of the county they were visiting. If it seems surprising that the couple should make this choice when only five miles from The Queen's childhood home, there was good reason. The Bury was by this time full of wounded servicemen and the casualties of enemy air raids.

At the outbreak of war, The Queen's two favourite Hertfordshire houses – the Bury and Hatfield House – were both offered to the authorities for use as hospitals. Elegant drawing rooms and magnificent banqueting halls gave up their grand furniture and trappings to make room for utility lockers, metal beds and rattling trolleys as the redoubtable nursing ladies of the Hertfordshire Red Cross and the Order of St John responded to the emergency.

Queen Elizabeth's brother David was a Lieutenant in the Hertfordshire Regiment (TA) when war broke out but, by 1940, had been transferred to top-secret work with the Ministry of Economic Warfare and the Special Operations Executive. Two years later he was sent to Washington to head our embassy's Political Warfare Mission and frequently carried messages between The King and President Roosevelt.

With her children also in America for the duration of the war, Rachel Bowes Lyon returned to the Bury to devote her time and energy to supporting the 50-bed hospital unit through which, by the end of the war, about 1,000 servicemen would be

(opposite page)
'Now have we got everyone in?' Convalescent servicemen crowd onto the staircase at the Bury to be photographed with Queen Elizabeth - an excellent billiards player herself, by the way.

(left) Leaving the military hospital at Hatfield House in 1940. With Queen Elizabeth are the matron, Miss Richardson, and – to the left of the group – James, 4th Marquess of Salisbury and, just behind him, his wife Lady Cicely.

nursed back to health. It was at her invitation, no doubt, that Queen Elizabeth made her one official wartime visit to the Bury. This was in October 1941, when she opened a physiotherapy unit provided with money that had been sent to her by a British-American War Relief Association in Seattle.

When life at the Bury was less exciting, Rachel Bowes Lyon helped to keep up patient morale by organising whist drives, dances and concerts by local entertainment groups. Topping the bill on special occasions were the songs and comic monologues of her close friend Joyce Grenfell and there was one visit from the 'Forces Sweetheart' Vera Lynn. According to Marjorie Ashurst of Walkern, who met her husband Jack while nursing him at the Bury, the dances were particularly popular with the patients despite their injuries – and she has never forgotten the challenge of trying to dance the quickstep with a partner who had one leg in plaster.

Although hospitalised, the servicemen remained subject to military discipline – which led to a certain amount of

'bull' and hasty tidying up whenever it became known that Mr David was due home on leave. However, apart from an occasional drinker stumbling home from the Strathmore Arms the worse for wear, there seems to have been little trouble. Indeed, the only time anyone can recall their host 'hitting the roof' was during visiting hours one Saturday when Mr David went out to inspect his beloved gardens

(below) With King George (in the foreground), Queen Elizabeth was at Hatfield again in 1942. They are seen walking from the Forest Lodge.

and caught a couple *in flagrante delicto* among the rhododendrons. A report to Army HQ seemed imminent until the embarrassed pair explained that they were married but hadn't seen each other for several weeks!

At the far more spacious Hatfield House, the emergency hospital was organised on a grander scale, treating more than 2,000 patients during the course of the war. The Cecils, 80 year old James, the 4th Marquess, and his wife Alice, moved into the East Wing, which they shared with an operating theatre, while the nursing staff coped with up to 300 patients at a time in the main part of the house.

Because of her close friendship with the Cecils, Queen Elizabeth made several wartime visits to the hospital, including at least one with The King. She seems also to have taken the opportunity for a brief break from her exhausting round of duties. After a visit in 1942, she told one of her

ladies-in-waiting: 'I knew it would do me good to come here – and it has.'

Not that she was likely to be much safer at Hatfield than in Buckingham Palace, where she and The King came close to losing their lives during one bombing raid. The de Havilland aircraft factory, just up the road from Hatfield House, was a sure target for enemy bombers – as on the dreadful day in October 1940 when four bombs from a Junkers 88 hit one of the workshops, killing 21 men. Another 13 residents – men, women and children – were killed later by two V1 'Flying Bombs.'

Neither Hatfield House nor St Paul's Walden Bury suffered direct hits, although, with Vauxhall Motors making tanks just over the county border in Luton, the Bury was also in a high risk area. In vain attempts to destroy the factory, German aircrews dropped 19 high explosive bombs and 1,100 incendiaries in the St Paul's Walden parish – most on open land, although a few properties in the vicinity were damaged by blast.

In September 1941, The King and Queen were in north Hertfordshire again to pay a surprise visit to Letchworth Garden City to meet men and women training for war work in the factories. Their tour of the Ascot Training Centre in Pixmore Avenue was part of a national campaign to recruit 100,000 women for war work, thus allowing more men to be released for active service.

Strict wartime security prevented newspapers from publishing advance notice of these 'hush hush' visits and even afterwards the *Hertfordshire Pictorial* felt obliged to describe the event as having taken place 'somewhere in the Home Counties.' Nevertheless, wartime restrictions did not affect the efficiency of the local bush telegraph, with the result that hundreds of residents turned out to welcome The King and Queen on what has turned out to be Queen Elizabeth's one and only visit to the world's first Garden City.

Welcoming crowds in Station Road, Letchworth in September 1941 when King George and Queen Elizabeth called in at the People's Hall.

'The constancy and the sacrifice . . .'

With the ending of hostilities one of Queen Elizabeth's first engagements within the county was to fulfil a long-delayed promise to review the 1st Battalion The Hertfordshire Regiment (Territorial Army) of which she had been Honorary Colonel since 1938 but whose officers and men she had not yet met.

Her appointment had been greeted with widespread enthusiasm in a county with a proud history of the volunteer spirit. The Hertfordshire Regiment (TA) was formed in 1908 from two earlier volunteer battalions, many of whose men had – like Queen Elizabeth's father – seen service in the South African War a few years earlier. In 1909, an application to adopt the county's ancient emblem of a hart for its regimental badge was given royal approval. Five years later, when the battalion was at its annual camp in Ashridge Park, orders came through to mobilise and in November 1914 – after just three months' further training – the Hertfordshire men sailed for France. The war claimed the lives of more than 900 of its officers and men, whose names are now commemorated on the regimental war memorial in All Saints' church, Hertford.

Not long after her appointment as their Honorary Colonel, The Queen was invited to review the 1st Battalion in the following summer of July 1939. Her reply, now among papers preserved in the County Record Office, has a touch of irony in view of events that followed. It regretted

Queen Elizabeth at County Hall, Hertford in July 1946, at a march past which included regimental old comrades from all over the county.

the review would not be possible in 1939 because a royal tour of Canada and the United States, planned for that year, had produced a congestion of engagements at home. Instead, Queen Elizabeth offered to come in the summer of 1940 – by which time, of course, war had been declared, the Battle of Britain had begun and the 1st Battalion was in Northumberland as part of the defences against a threatened German invasion.

For most of the Second World War the battalion had to endure what were described by one officer as 'times of drudgery, disillusion, boredom and frustration' as they remained on defence duties year after year, first in England and then Gibraltar. It wasn't until August 1944 that they went into battle. During their four months of front-line service in Italy, more than 100 officers and men were killed in action as the 1st Battalion fought its way

Officers of the Hertfordshire Regiment and the 5th Battalion Beds and Herts Regiment kneel before Queen Elizabeth to receive new colours, at County Hall, Hertford in October 1953.

A proud display of medals as old comrades of The Beds and Herts parade for their Colonel-in-Chief when the regiment was granted the Freedom of Hertford in 1969.

through the mountains from the Arno river to the Po. Among its several battle honours, none was better won than 'Gothic Line', which commemorates the battalion's signal contribution to the breaking of the formidable German defences north of Florence in September 1944.

The regiment's 2nd Battalion – formed when war became imminent – took part in the D-Day landings as the 'core battalion' of No 9 Beach Group. The group was responsible for clearing 12,000 unexploded mines from their sector of the Normandy beaches and claimed the record for 'managing' the greatest number of men, vehicles and equipment ashore from landing craft in one day. However, no sooner was this vital work over than 2nd

Battalion suffered what Queen Elizabeth later described as 'a sad reward and a most melancholy fate'. Almost overnight it was disbanded and its men split up and sent to reinforce other units in the advance across north-west Europe to Berlin.

The Queen's sympathetic remarks were made when she was finally able to review her regiment at Hertford in July 1946 – some eight years after receiving the original invitation! Unfortunately, the 1st Battalion were unable to attend as a unit, since they were serving in troubled Palestine at the time. Even so, nearly 3,000 servicemen, veterans and cadets took part in the Service of Thanksgiving and march past. In a surprisingly long speech, as if to make amends for the years the war had kept them apart, their Honorary Colonel charted her regiment's history in some detail, saying it had a record of service of which it could be proud.

'On such a day as this we should recall with gratitude and with pride the constancy and the sacrifice made by the men of Hertfordshire. They typify in their service the spirit of all Englishmen who are ready when their country is in peril to give all that they have without thought for themselves. I rejoice to learn that it is proposed to continue a Territorial force which will offer comradeship and the opportunity of service to all who join it.'

It is appropriate here also to recall Queen Elizabeth's years as Colonel-in-Chief of The Bedfordshire and Hertfordshire Regiment, in which many other local men served with distinction and bravery in both World Wars and later campaigns. Following that first review in 1946, Queen Elizabeth honoured both regiments at other historic ceremonies before they lost their individual identities in the amalgamations that came with the cuts in our Armed Forces. However, their royal patron retains a strong link with Hertfordshire's present-day soldiers as Colonel-in-Chief of the Royal Anglian Regiment in which many successors to the two local regiments now serve.

Faster than a Meteor

'A wonderful, exhilarating experience.
A day I shall remember for always.'

Although her first aircraft flight – to Brussels in 1935 – had been a bumpy one that left her suffering from airsickness, Queen Elizabeth was to develop a passion for flying that reached its zenith when she celebrated her 85th birthday by making a supersonic trip on the flight deck of Concorde. However, there had been earlier indications of this lust for speed when she and Princess Margaret made their first trip in a jet aircraft, from the de Havilland aerodrome at Hatfield in May 1952.

After the tragically early death of King George VI in February of that year, his widow assumed the title by which she will be best remembered – Queen Elizabeth The Queen Mother. Some 12 weeks after the King's funeral, Queen Elizabeth began gently to resume public life. Among those helping her through this sad time were her great friends Bobbety and Betty at Hatfield House. And it was Lord and Lady Salisbury who set the ball rolling for her flight in Britain's pioneer jet airliner, the de Havilland Comet I.

Also in the party that day were Sir Geoffrey and Lady de Havilland, the Chairman of BOAC Sir Miles Thomas and Group Captain Peter Townsend, plus – at The Queen Mother's insistence – the two chauffeurs who had driven them to the airfield. The party was welcomed on board by Group Captain John 'Cats Eyes' Cunningham, the wartime nightfighter ace who, as de Havilland's chief test pilot, had recently completed the Comet's proving trials.

For The Queen Mother's treat, he had prepared a 1,850 mile flight plan to take them on a spectacular four-hour trip over The Alps and along the French Riviera coastline. Halfway through the journey, when the royal guests had enjoyed their first meal at 40,000 feet, John Cunningham handed the controls to his co-pilot Peter Bugge and invited Queen Elizabeth onto the flight-deck to try her hand at flying the new machine.

Having sat in Cunningham's seat for a while, holding the airliner on a steady course, it became apparent that Her Majesty was rather more interested in their speed. Told it was about 500 miles an hour, she asked: 'Is that as fast as a Meteor fighter can fly?'

'Not quite, Ma'am,' the test pilot replied.

'Well, can we make it go faster than a Meteor?' Queen Elizabeth persisted.

A slightly puzzled John Cunningham assured her that they could and, with their guest still at the controls, the crew put the aircraft into a shallow descent, during which the needle on the Mach indicator crept to just short of the maximum speed allowed when carrying passengers. At just over Mach 0.8 the test pilot was able to tell his guest: 'There you are, Ma'am. You are now flying faster than a Meteor.'

'Oh, good!' came the reply. 'I shall

have enormous pleasure in telling them this.' It turned out that Queen Elizabeth was due at the annual dinner of 600 Squadron of the Royal Auxiliary Air Force that week and wanted to be able to report that their Honorary Air Commodore had flown faster than any of the pilots in their Meteor squadron!

A dramatic account of this little adventure appeared later in the autobiography of BOAC's Chairman, Sir Miles Thomas, who had been taking photographs on the flight deck at the time. In *Out On A Wing* (1964), he wrote: 'The mach needle crept towards the coloured danger sector and suddenly the Comet began to porpoise (an undulating movement). Not violently but just enough to indicate that we had reached the limit of her aerodynamic stability . . . That trip was, of course, before the cataclysmic crashes that the Comets later suffered through structural weakness, and had that

porpoising gone on much longer, the wracking on the structure could well have precipitated a rupture of the skin of the kind that caused the subsequent tragedies. I still shudder every time I think of that flight.'

John Cunningham, now living in retirement at Kinsbourne Green, near Harpenden, read Sir Miles' version of the trip with what might be described as 'amused disdain'. He told the author that there were no shudders from the aircraft or its occupants that day. The Comet had achieved its extra speed quite smoothly and without any problems. As for The Queen Mother – her only comment, as she rejoined the others, was: 'We're going to find the Vikings of the Royal Flight very slow after this!'

Clearly elated by the trip, Her Majesty fired off a triumphant telegram to 600 Squadron as soon as she arrived home.

In a hand-written letter received by

Still dressed in black during the period of official mourning for King George VI, Queen Elizabeth receives a nosegay from young Anne de Havilland after the high-speed flight. Sir Miles Thomas is on the aircraft steps.

Beneath the Comet's tail, Sir Geoffrey de Havilland looks on as The Queen Mother thanks test pilot John Cunningham, while a relaxed Princess Margaret, feet crossed, has a few final words with Sir Miles Thomas. The factory and aerodrome at Hatfield, last owned by British Aerospace, closed in 1994 – sixty years after the first de Havilland aircraft were built there.

John Cunningham the next day, The Queen Mother describes the flight as: 'A wonderful, exhilarating experience. A day I shall remember for always.' Accompanying the letter was a small package. It contained a set of gold cuff links engraved with the initials 'ER'.

Since then, Queen Elizabeth's liking for being 'up front' during a flight has provided memorable moments for a good many aircrews. Another former Hatfield pilot and captain with The Queen's Flight recalls finding her standing alongside him on the flight deck as they were about to make their descent. Wondering how best to persuade her to return to her seat before the landing, he ventured the tactful comment: 'Well, Ma'am, I hope everyone's sitting down with their seat belts on.' On hearing this, Queen Elizabeth turned round and announced in ringing tones of which any air steward would be proud: 'The captain wants you all to sit down and fasten your seat belts.' Then she turned back and continued to supervise the landing. She was 83 at the time.

1955

The genial soldier-courtier

Lieutenant-Colonel Sir Martin Gilliat
GCVO, MBE, DL

A Hertfordshire army officer and war hero who joined the staff of Clarence House in 1955 and stayed for four decades, Lieutenant-Colonel Sir Martin Gilliat is remembered as the courtier who played a decisive role in transforming Queen Elizabeth's image from that of grieving widow into the 'Queen Mum' figure that has made her the best-loved ambassadress of the British Monarchy.

Chorleywood Cedars, near Rickmansworth, Frogmore Hall and The Manor House at Welwyn.

When he joined The Queen Mother's household, Sir Martin decided to keep a property in Hertfordshire and bought 'Appletrees', a 17th century timber-framed house backing onto the river Mimram in Welwyn village. It remained his home for

Appletrees, Sir Martin's Elizabethan house in Mill Lane, Welwyn, his home for nearly 40 years.

Like his employer – as he often described his royal mistress – Sir Martin was descended from Hertfordshire's landed gentry. His parents came from two banking families of whom one member – a grandfather – was Governor of the Bank of England. Their estates have included

40 years until he moved to London shortly before his death in 1993 at the age of 80.

The first half of this soldier-courtier's life now reads like one of those G.A. Henty adventure stories of Empire-building heroes, whose exploits so enthralled schoolboys of Sir Martin's generation. Adventure and danger seemed to run in his family. His father, Lt-Colonel John Babington Gilliat, won the DSO for bravery in the South African War and his elder brother died after being mauled by a tiger while serving with the Royals in India.

After Eton and Sandhurst the young Gilliat was commissioned into The King's Royal Rifle Corps and at the outbreak of war was soon in France with the British Expeditionary Force. By the fall of Calais in 1940 all his battalion had been either killed or captured and, as the Dunkirk evacuation began, he was one of hundreds of prisoners being force-marched across

France to Germany. He escaped twice during the journey only to be recaptured.

Later, Gilliat made more escape attempts from various prison camps, including one by tunnel and another in which he and 28 other officers dodged heavy gunfire to scale a perimeter fence using climbing frames and ladders that they had built secretly. That time he was at liberty for a fortnight. Eventually, he was classified as a persistent escaper and sent to the infamous Colditz Castle where he remained until the prison stronghold was liberated in 1945.

However, the soldier Gilliat's brushes with danger did not end with the war. In 1947, while serving in Delhi as a military secretary to India's last Viceroy, Earl Mountbatten, his car was attacked by rioters and he was shot in the neck. Trapped inside with a companion and their dead driver he suffered heavy loss of blood before rescuers arrived and rushed him to hospital just in time to save his life.

Following other more peaceful tours of duty, Col Gilliat became Assistant Private Secretary to The Queen Mother in 1955. Within a year he was appointed Private Secretary and Equerry 'on a trial basis'. Knighted for his services in 1962, Sir Martin would joke 30 years on that he was still waiting to hear whether the job would be made permanent.

A genial bachelor figure, Sir Martin shared his employer's love of the Turf and the Theatre; he owned his own string of racehorses and was an 'angel' investor in many West End shows. As a result, he became not only The Queen Mother's equerry, but her devoted companion and adviser as well.

On Her Majesty's 80th birthday – he suggested that it might be a good time for him to retire; to which Queen Elizabeth swiftly responded that she was 13 years older than him and she had no intention of retiring. He stayed, of course, to continue as the popular central figure of her household for another decade.

Arriving at Bishop's Stortford College by helicopter in 1968 to be greeted by the Lord Lieutenant, Major General Sir George Burns, with the tall figure of Sir Martin Gilliat looking on with Lady Rankin, the Queen Mother's lady-in-waiting.

1955

Home and school

'The close partnership'

With education and the welfare of young people high on The Queen Mother's list of interests, one of Sir Martin Gilliat's first jobs at Clarence House was to help organise her visit to a new Hertfordshire school that was to become a prototype for many of Britain's post-war educational buildings.

Having had to accommodate three new towns and several London 'overspill' developments within a few years, Hertfordshire's urgent need for more schools provided the County Council with what was probably the biggest challenge in its history. In the 20 years up to 1951, the county's population had doubled; the school leaving age had been raised and there was also a 'baby boom'. It was esti-

mated that, for primary education alone, Hertfordshire would need 175 new schools by 1960.

Faced with these extreme demands the Education and Architect's departments pooled their resources to produce a school-building programme that was later acknowledged as 'a brilliant example of local initiative'. Sharing the honours for this were John Newsom, the County's forward-thinking Education Officer, who was later knighted for his services, the County Architect Charles Aslin and a young architect named Stirrat Johnson-Marshall, who went on to become chief architect to the Ministry of Education. These men created buildings like the one opened by Queen Elizabeth at Hitchin in March 1955.

It was at this opening that Queen Elizabeth revealed her firm views about the importance of parental support for schools – views just as topical today. Having expressed admiration for the way the county was overcoming its education problems with the help of buildings like Hitchin's 'beautiful new school', she added:

'However, no school depends for its success on the quality of its buildings alone. Education is essentially a personal matter in which teachers, pupils and parents must all play their part . . . I hope very much that the parents will take a real interest in what is being taught here and will play an increasing part in the life of the school, so that their children may be conscious of the close partnership which should exist between home and school.'

Similar views were expressed in 1967 when The Queen Mother went to see a new secondary school built at Wheathampstead to serve rural communities in north-western Hertfordshire, including Whitwell and St Paul's Walden.

Queen Elizabeth's interest in Hertfordshire's schools began in 1925 when, as Duchess of York, she and The Duke went to Bushey for the annual prize-giving at 'The Caley', otherwise the Royal Caledonian Schools, where more than 10,000 children of Scottish servicemen and needy Scottish families had been educated. At the time, The Duke was Chief of the Scottish Clans Association and, with her own strong Scottish ancestry, it was hardly surprising that The Queen Mother should later become Patroness, returning several times to celebrate important events in The Caley's history.

In 1995, principally because of the cuts in Britain's Armed Forces, the residential facilities at Bushey were closed and the building sold to the Purcell School of Music. However, Queen Elizabeth remains Patroness of The Caley's new Educational Trust, which is dedicated to helping chil-

dren of Scottish servicemen and needy Scottish families south of the border.

When Hertford Grammar School celebrated its 350th anniversary in 1967, Queen Elizabeth combined her visit there with a parade held on the school playing fields to mark the laying-up of the colours of the 1st Battalion The Hertfordshire Regiment. That same year, with education authorities under government pressure to abolish grammar schools, the school was renamed the Richard Hale School after the City of London merchant who founded it. Two years later, it received a second royal visit when The Queen Mother returned to accept the Freedom of Hertford in her new role as Colonel-in-Chief of the Royal Anglian Regiment.

There's little doubt that Her Majesty's most spectacular arrival at a school was on a sunny May day in 1968, when she flew to the eastern boundaries of the county to 'drop in' for the centenary celebrations of Bishop's Stortford College. Guests lining the College's Middle Green playing field applauded as a bright red helicopter of The Queen's Flight swept in low over the library block to land neatly in their midst. 'Thank you for your kind welcome,' she said later. 'Despite my rather unorthodox arrival, landing as I did almost literally at your feet!'

Excited children surround the royal car at the opening of Hitchin High School for Girls in 1955. The school later became co-educational and is now called The Priory School.

At Hitchin Youth Centre in 1969 and a chat with Alan James, aged 17, whose group The Limit answered a royal command for music by playing 'On A Wonderful Day Like Today.'

1956

'A certain kind of courage'

Welcoming Londoners to the first new town

At the time of Queen Elizabeth's birth, Stevenage was a small market town of 4,000 people. Like Baldock, a few miles to the north, the original town possesses a wide and attractive High Street where markets and fairs have been held for centuries; a street once part of the Great North Road and still lined with Georgian houses and coaching inns

the end of the Second World War as Britain buckled down to the task of providing new housing and work for families whose lives and homes had been devastated by bombing. Incredibly, nine out of ten London homes had been either damaged or destroyed. The government decided that the only way out of the crisis was to build ten new towns in the Home Counties – and Stevenage was selected as

from the days when much of its prosperity depended on passing traffic. For most residents at the turn of the century their only sight of royalty had been a fleeting one – as kings, queens, princes and princesses swept through on their way to more exciting places.

As the century ends, Stevenage's population has increased somewhat – to 76,000. The expansion began shortly after the site for the first. The plan, which was met with strong but fruitless opposition from local residents, covered 6,000 acres and affected about 100 farms, 20 of which disappeared altogether.

By the mid-1950s, with three neighbourhoods complete, the Development Corporation turned its attention to the town centre and the new parish church of St Andrew and St George. Work there had only just begun when The Queen Mother paid her first visit one wet Saturday in July 1956. In the middle of a muddy building site, on an improvised stage of planks and scaffolding, her diminutive figure all but disappeared behind the large foundation stone she had been invited to lay.

Many who defied the rain to cheer her were people with whom she had a special affinity; Londoners who, like her own family, had refused to leave the capital,

even during the worst of the Blitz, young couples who had had to spend their first married years in grim lodgings that offered little space, comfort or privacy. So when the chance came to head for the countryside and breathe life into England's first post-war new town it seemed almost heaven-sent. Yet the move itself called for a certain kind of courage which The Queen Mother likened to the resolution of the pioneers who had founded the Greek City States 2,500 years earlier:

A royal handshake for the rector's daughter, Louise Cordingley (9) after presenting Queen Elizabeth with a bouquet - and in the background (right) a young Richard Whitmore looking on!

Queen Elizabeth arriving at 79 Broad Oak Way, the home of Ken and Gina Biggs, having asked to meet a new town family. The Biggs family spent some time with their royal visitor, having delayed the start of their summer holiday so that they could show her round their home.

'There, people with no previous knowledge or experience of civic life had the faith and far-sightedness to unite and start a new and wonderful civilisation,' she told the crowd. 'For them, the centre of life was the market place, where they met, held discussions and decided on the future of the state. In your new town I trust that the church which is to be built here will, with its civic centre, provide for parishioners a rallying point where the centre of the new community life will grow and prosper.'

With Hertfordshire obliged to accommodate three of the ten new towns – at Stevenage, Hatfield and Hemel Hempstead – the burden on the St Albans diocesan administrators was heavier than for most. Much of it fell on the shoulders of the man conducting the service that day, the 6th Bishop of St Albans, Michael Gresford Jones. The Stevenage church was only one of 40 places of worship, large and small, that had to be built and staffed for the new towns and other overspill areas in his diocese. Bishop Gresford Jones was at the

helm throughout this testing period until his retirement in 1970, a quiet, pastoral bishop and an excellent administrator who came along just when one was needed.

Some years later, the church received a valuable memento from its royal patron. At Stevenage again in 1960 to celebrate its completion and consecration, The Queen Mother discovered that the clergy had little or no communion plate for their services and promptly arranged for a rare George III silver communion set to be provided on permanent loan from the royal vaults.

With its huge arches of pre-cast concrete, its open tower and electronic chimes, St Andrew's and St George's raised quite a few eyebrows when it went up. One wonders how many would have guessed then that as Stevenage celebrated its 50th anniversary in 1996, the building would be singled out for praise by English Heritage, who commended the architects for the skilful way they had 'translated the Gothic style into a modern language.'

(right) In 1984, more than 30 years after the Comet flight, Queen Elizabeth met her 'instructor' Group Captain Cunningham (left) at the Silver Jubilee celebrations of the de Havilland Mosquito Aircraft Museum at Salisbury Hall, London Colney.

'Queen Mother', the new patio rose introduced to celebrate Queen Elizabeth's 90th birthday.

At Hitchin to open The
Queen Mother Theatre in
1983. With Queen
Elizabeth are Sir George
Burns and Founder
President of the theatre,
Richard Whitmore.

(right) Signing the visitor's
book.

1961

'To be amongst friends . . .'

*'A visit to Hertfordshire is very much a
return home and to be in St Albans is, I feel,
to be amongst friends.'*

If ever there was an appropriate year for The Queen Mother to become an Honorary Freeman of St Albans it was 1961. For the City Council had just made headlines by becoming the first local authority in England with a Mayor and a Town Clerk who were both women. Indeed, the clerk Miss Betty Entwistle was the only woman town clerk in the country at that time – so it was hardly surprising that 'distinguished

*Queen Elizabeth pauses for
the National Anthem before
going into St Albans' Town
Hall to receive the Freedom
of the City from the Mayor,
Dr Elsie Toms, in April
1961.*

In conversation with the Mayor at a lunch held in Batchwood Hall before the 'Freedom' ceremony.

Bishop of St Albans, the Rt Rev Michael Furse, was chosen to be one of Queen Elizabeth's supporting bishops at the Coronation. At the time, the city's flourishing print industry had presented each of the two young princesses with a specially-bound bible: a gesture not forgotten by their mother nearly 25 years later when she told the company: 'I know how highly The Queen and my daughter Margaret treasure those bibles, bound in St Albans, which were given to them at the time of The King's Coronation.'

women' featured prominently in the Town Hall speeches that April afternoon. Those who watched Queen Elizabeth receiving the freedom scroll in its silver and crystal glass casket remember her amusement when 'Mr Mayor' – the former headmistress Dr Elsie Toms – recalled a list of earlier visits to St Albans by notable female monarchs, not least Queen Boadicea, whose marauding army had burnt down most of the Roman city in AD 61!

In her reply, their new Freeman said few cities could boast a background of such vivid interest and colourful tradition as St Albans. Ancient Britons, Romans, Saxons and Normans; all the influences of 2,000 years and more had left their mark and bequeathed something to the culture and heritage of the city. Expressing her pride in joining the Company of Freemen, Queen Elizabeth said she valued the honour all the more because – 'A visit to Hertfordshire is very much a return home and to be in St Albans is, I feel, to be amongst friends.'

An early example of that friendship had occurred in 1937 when the then

Recalling that St Albans had been 'the scene of mighty triumphs, grievous trials, of pillage and destruction, and of heroic enterprise', The Queen Mother was probably remembering her visit in 1948 when great events in the city's history were recreated at a 'millenary pageant' performed on the site of the Roman city of Verulamium. Set against a spectacular backdrop of the lake and magnificent hilltop cathedral, the pageant could not have had a more perfect setting.

Alban was said to have been converted to Christianity by a priest he was sheltering from persecution. He became the first of Britain's Christian martyrs, giving the Cathedral and Abbey Church the rare distinction of protecting the precise spot where he was sacrificed for his faith. Although a shrine was erected almost immediately after

vives today with its beautifully proportioned tower rising nearly 150 feet above the city. It was to celebrate the 900th Anniversary of the founding of this abbey that The Queen Mother came to St Albans in 1977. A busy year for the citizens who, as well as joining the rest of the nation in celebrating The Queen's Silver Jubilee, staged a series of local celebrations throughout the year under the rather trendy umbrella title of FestAlban.

1977 also marked the first centenary of St Albans as a diocese; for it is a strange fact of Church history that the city with a cathedral containing one of England's most important shrines came into its own as a diocese only towards the end of the last century, giving the abbey the status of a cathedral. Thomas Claughton's enthronment as the first Bishop of St Albans in 1877, coincided with the granting of a royal charter that gave St Albans city status.

(centre) The casket, of silver and crystal glass, was made by a St Albans' silversmith, Mr John Webb. The central mount carries the city's shield with the Bowes Lyon coat of arms on the end cap.

Watched by a smiling Mayor, Queen Elizabeth holds up her casket and scroll after accepting the Freedom of the City.

Alban's execution, nothing more was built on the site until a small monastery appeared about 150 years later.

The first abbey was founded in the eighth-century by the Mercian King Offa and that was replaced in 1077 when the Normans built the splendid abbey that sur-

Like most of England's great shrines, the original 14th century monument to St Alban was demolished at the time of Henry VIII's dissolution of the monasteries. The reliquary containing the martyr's bones was never found but – by a stroke of good fortune – much of the pedestal on

(next page) The restored shrine of the first Christian martyr, St Alban, focal point of the city's cathedral.

which it stood was discovered during maintenance work in 1847 and 1872. The pedestal's shattered pieces – more than 2,000 fragments in all – had been discarded as rubble and used with other materials to block off the abbey's Lady Chapel.

However, being of Purbeck marble they were quite easy for experts to identify and, under the supervision of the church architect Sir Gilbert Scott, the jigsaw of broken pieces was eventually rebuilt by a local stonemason, Mr Charles Fisher.

By the early 1990s the restored shrine was showing signs of wear and instability, so in 1991 it was dismantled once more. Each fragment was stripped of its Victorian adhesive and the grime and grease of a century carefully cleaned away. This time, perhaps not to the approval of all traditionalists, new panes and pillars made of modern materials were added to represent those parts of the shrine that have never been found and – to improve stability – the whole pedestal was rebuilt around a light metal frame, cleverly constructed so that it cannot be seen from the outside. Finally, the monument was topped by a colourful replica of the embroidered silk canopies that were used to decorate important shrines in monastic days.

Thirty years earlier, before all the pageantry of the Town Hall ceremony at which she received the Freedom of the City, Queen Elizabeth had paid a private visit to the abbey, where she spent some time kneeling in prayer at the Shrine of St Alban. Since then she has made several more visits to what she clearly considers to be an important point of her Christian worship. So it was no surprise when she accepted the city's invitation to be at the special Evensong in May 1993, when the shrine – restored to more than its former glory – was rehallowed in readiness for Christian pilgrims of the new millennium.

1961

'We have lost our best friend'

Sir David Bowes Lyon (1902–1961)

Sadly, Queen Elizabeth's memorable day at St Albans in April 1961 was also the last occasion at which Sir David Bowes Lyon welcomed his sister to the county in his official role as Lord Lieutenant of Hertfordshire.

In July that year, some three months after the visit, Sir David suffered a severe asthma attack. He appeared to recover and a few weeks later was well enough to go on holiday with his family to Scotland, joining Queen Elizabeth at Birkhall, her house on the Balmoral estate, where The Queen and Prince Philip were also on holiday. It was at Birkhall on 13th September that Sir David had a further attack and died; at 59, he was the second dearly loved man in The Queen Mother's life to suffer a sudden and untimely death.

Like all Bowes Lyon boys, Sir David had been educated at Eton before going to Magdalen College, Oxford and then to the City to begin his business career as a merchant banker. Later, he widened his interests to serve on the boards of a number of well-known banking and city institutions, including *The Times* Publishing Company, Martins Bank, Cunard and Dunlop.

Sir David's long-standing interest in the welfare of his home county led to his appointment as High Sheriff of Hertfordshire in 1950 and Lord Lieutenant in 1952, a post he held until his death. He was knighted in 1959. It is hardly surprising that, after his own family, Sir David's death was felt most keenly by the people of the county and St Paul's Walden in particular where – like his father the Earl of Strathmore before him – he had been a popular squire.

Both David and Rachel Bowes Lyon liked nothing more than to be out and

about among Hertfordshire people, whether at the county's agricultural show, visiting a youth club or distributing awards for the Best Kept Village Competition. While Lady Bowes Lyon served for the community as Justice of the Peace and member of both Hertfordshire County Council and Hitchin Rural Council, her husband devoted much of his spare time to helping the young people, particularly those in the nearby new town of Stevenage. When told of Sir David's death, the Secretary of Stevenage Youth Trust, Mr R.S. McDougall, said with sad simplicity:

St Paul's Walden Bury as Sir David Bowes Lyon left it in 1961, showing the beech hedges which he planted either side of the great walk.

A brotherly escort for 'The Queen Mother at the opening of the High School for Girls, Hitchin in 1956.

had also achieved remarkable success growing rhododendrons and azaleas. At this time the Bury's thriving market garden business sometimes led Lady Bowes Lyon to assume the unlikely role of a stallholder on Hitchin Market, serving customers with 'fruit and veg' grown in the Bury's kitchen garden!

A telling illustration of the Bowes Lyons' delight in simple local pleasures occurred during the Coronation celebrations of 2nd June 1953. Having taken part in the great event at Westminster Abbey they hurried back to St Paul's Walden to join fellow parishioners in a marquee for a whopping Coronation Supper.

Sadly, it was only eight years later that The Queen, Prince Philip and The Queen Mother joined Lady Bowes Lyon and her family at Sir David's funeral service following his death in Scotland. The service was divided into two parts. The first was held at St Kentigern's church, Ballater, Aberdeenshire, after which Sir David's body was brought back to Hertfordshire on the royal train for burial at St Paul's Walden.

Estate tenants and staff joined the family for the short service of committal at All Saints, after which Sir David was laid to rest in the churchyard – just across the lane from the house and gardens where the two Benjamins had spent their childhood and where he had later worked so hard to restore the estate to its former glory.

Those who came later to pay their respects found the church path banked with more than 300 floral tributes. From 'Lilibet and Philip', from 'Elizabeth' and others of the Royal Family; from banking and city institutions, national and local authorities, tenant farmers, retired estate workers and elderly widows. Elegant wreaths but also many simple sprays of those local flowers that had given such delight to the public-spirited Hertfordshire knight with gifted green fingers.

'We have lost our first Chairman and our best friend.' Some years later that friend was remembered when his name was given to Bowes Lyon House, a splendid building that when opened in 1965, was the largest purpose-built youth centre in the country.

Having shared The Queen Mother's love of gardening – they had both been President of the Royal Horticultural Society – Sir David worked hard to restore the St Paul's Walden Bury gardens to the style in which they had been laid out by Edward Gilbert in the early 18th century, with attractive woodland areas and walks featuring a host of exotic trees, temples and statues. 'A delightful combination of the formal and informal,' said *The Times*, recalling that although the Bury stands on inhospitable clay soil – a challenge to the finest gardener – Sir David had managed to grow avenues of superb beech trees and hedges (planted with his own hands) and

1966

A royal rosarian

With the possible exception of horse racing, The Queen Mother's most pleasurable hobby has been to grow roses. Her homes at Royal Lodge, Windsor and the Castle of Mey bear witness to that. The Royal Lodge rose garden, which she and King George helped to rebuild with their own hands in the 1930s, is regarded as one of the finest in the country.

With such a background it was hardly surprising that Queen Elizabeth should find herself invited to become Patron of the Royal National Rose Society, a post she has held since 1965 and which brought her to Hertfordshire the following year, when she paid a private visit to the society's headquarters at Chiswell Green, near St Albans.

The Gardens of the Rose, as they are now known, began their life in 1960 after the RNRS had to leave its London offices because of redevelopment. The society bought the former farmhouse of Bone Hill and its small estate for little more than £30,000 and during the following four decades developed the extensive display and trial grounds that now attract thousands of admiring visitors every year.

The Queen Mother Rose Garden, opened in 1989, is a popular feature at Chiswell Green, although displays of roses bearing their patron's name can be found all over the grounds – for nobody has had more species named after them than The Queen Mother.

According to the Hertfordshire rosarian Peter Harkness, whose family runs the world-renowned rose nursery and gardens at Hitchin, the first to bear her name was *Duchess of York*, a large-flowered hybrid tea rose in deep golden yellow

with tangerine centre, produced by Sandy Dickson of Belfast in 1925. Following *Duchess of York* came *Elizabeth*, launched by Letts of Suffolk to celebrate Coronation Year in 1937. Since the war, four new roses have borne The Queen Mother's title, though one only briefly, after it was decided that Her Majesty's name should be withdrawn for reasons of etiquette. The rose in question was a lovely pink cluster-

Not surprisingly, roses featured in the bouquet presented to the Queen by Isobel Harkness of the Hitchin rose-growing family, at the town's Festival of Britain Pageant in 1951.

enthusiasts, the grower and his agent suggested changing it to *The Queen Mother* but the idea was rejected on the grounds that using a royal title as second choice was hardly fitting!

This left the field wide open once more and in 1959 Stedman of Peterborough came out with a Mark II version of *The Queen Mother* – another pink cluster-flowered floribunda similar to the original *August Seebauer* but, in Peter Harkness's opinion, not as good. Probably the most famous 'Queen Mum' rose was introduced five years later in 1964 by another Northern Ireland grower, Sam McGredy. With its lovely blend of salmon, orange and pink, *Elizabeth of Glamis* carried off the National Rose Society's top award and is still as popular as it was on the day it was introduced.

The most recent new variety to be named after the royal rosarian brings a final twist to the story. During Queen Elizabeth's 90th birthday celebrations, a dainty pink patio rose was introduced at the 1990 Chelsea Flower Show.

Christened – yet again – *Queen Mother*, it was developed in north Germany by Wilhelm Kordes, the grower whose earlier *August Seebauer* had been refused the name 40 years before. 'And,' observed Peter Harkness, 'of all the roses named after The Queen Mother, I think this is the best in growth and flower – a delightful addition to any garden.'

Meeting rosarian Jack Harkness (left), brother of Peter, who was displaying the first examples of his breeding work at the RNRS summer show in 1966. The Society's President, Fred Gibson, is on the right.

flowered floribunda, promoted in the 1950s by Henry Morse of Norfolk who had obtained it from Germany where it had been introduced during the war as *August Seebauer*. Convinced that this Teutonic name wouldn't appeal to British

(right) Talking roses, Queen Elizabeth snapped during a private visit to the RNRS gardens at Chiswell Green in 1966.

1968 & 1983

'The theatre is irresistible'

(Matthew Arnold 1822–1888)

Amongst The Queen Mother's numerous biographers are one or two who have floated the thought that Elizabeth Bowes Lyon might well have become an actress, even a Gaiety Girl, had Fate not led her along a different path. Certainly, she grew up at a time when the acting profession had become 'respectable', resulting in a good many bright young gels from the aristocracy heading for the stage.

The young Elizabeth's childhood passion for dressing up is well-documented; so are the Christmas musical festivities at the Bury which featured her lively renditions of popular cockney music hall songs – sometimes imaginatively adapted to include the people present. In later years, of course, distinguished house guests have reported going through agonies to satisfy The Queen Mother's appetite for charades.

In fact, the job Queen Elizabeth has done so well for so long, that of making The Personal Appearance, frequently calls for considerable acting skills in itself – which could be why she always refers to her familiar stole, handbag and jewellery as 'my props'.

In Hertfordshire, she has given enthusiastic support to two enterprising amateur drama groups who have succeeded in building and running their own theatres. In 1968 she went to St Albans to see the Company of Ten's gala production of *The Recruiting Officer*, which celebrated the opening of the Abbey Theatre, and in

1983 she was at Hitchin to give her name to the Queen Mother Theatre, home of the Bancroft Players and the only theatre in the country to bear her name.

Perhaps it's not surprising that, as Founder President and Trustee of the Queen Mother Theatre, this author finds himself sharing similar memories to those of his opposite number at St Albans – the Company of Ten's President, Terry Newell. Once a royal visit has been agreed it is the

Meeting the cast of the Company of Ten's production of 'The Recruiting Officer' to inaugurate the Abbey Theatre at St Albans in 1968.

visitors who dictate the date they will come. So, for a group of volunteers building a theatre there can be problems if the date 'suggested' is rather earlier than they had planned.

In his book *Ten of the Best* Terry Newell provides some splendid examples of Sir Martin Gilliat's great style when advising on these events:

'As Clarence House has always stressed the need for informality we wrote and enquired whether Her Majesty would like to partake of coffee and light refreshments during the intervals. We were a little disconcerted to be advised by return post that our guest would appreciate champagne and that she was particularly fond of Veuve Cliquot. Happily that august house covered the matter by donating a crate (sic) of their best vintage which was enjoyed equally by Her Majesty and many

of her subjects.'

Sir Martin also suggested that, to comfortably accommodate the full ball-gown their guest would be wearing, the organisers might do well to ensure that seat C9 was made a little wider than the others and that 11 seats were taken out of the row in front in order to make access and viewing easier. The Company of Ten complied, of course, and seat C9 – three inches wider than the rest – is still there today, bearing the name of its illustrious first occupant.

It was during her July stay at St Paul's

Leaving the Abbey Theatre escorted by the Company of Ten's President, Terry Newell and the Lord Lieutenant of Hertfordshire, Sir George Burns.

Walden that The Queen Mother went to inaugurate the Bancroft Players' theatre at Hitchin. Because the building wasn't due to open until September, the obligatory champagne reception this time took place in a seatless auditorium, where Queen Elizabeth met some 300 members and patrons who had helped with the project.

Those of us involved with planning the day recall with a wry smile Sir Martin's discreet and serious reminder that Her Majesty was now well into her eighties and that we should be prepared lest some sudden indisposition force her to shorten her visit or, even worse, to cancel it altogether. In fact, the event over-ran by nearly an hour as our octogenarian visitor ploughed merrily on, stopping to chat with all and sundry in every corner of the theatre – concluding with a brisk walkabout among the hundreds waiting outside to see her.

To celebrate The Queen Mother's 90th birthday, we had the idea of compiling a revue – *Her Favourite Things* – based on items from shows that this avid theatregoer had particularly enjoyed over the

After the opening of the Queen Mother Theatre, Richard Whitmore, Founder President, bids farewell to Queen Elizabeth.

years. A letter to Clarence House seeking guidance on this subject produced the customary reply by return. Top of the list were the Crazy Gang; then, Gilbert and Sullivan, Noel Coward's plays and 'the best of the American musicals of the immediate post World War II period.'

As work began selecting songs and sketches to reflect these choices, we were surprised by a second letter from Clarence House a fortnight later. Queen Elizabeth had been having some further thoughts, wrote Sir Martin. She wondered whether we might like to include her favourite jazz

numbers as well: *Alexander's Rag Time Band, Waiting for the Robert E. Lee* and *When the Midnight Choo Choo leaves for Alabam!*

The tabloid press had a field day with that one.

'It's The Queen Momma' yelled the *Sun*. 'Royal Swinger Says: I'm Crazy About All That Jazz!'

The show was a sell-out, despite disappointment that the royal star herself was unable to come because of a long-standing 90th birthday engagement at Windsor.

1969

The secret in the handbag

Although the Hertford-shire division of the St John Ambulance Brigade had been formed since the 1930s, their review by The Queen Mother at Hatfield in May 1969 was the first ever by a royal patron. It also turned MBE. He was County Commissioner and a Knight of the Order of St John and he had played a significant role in arranging the inspection. Giving the Brigade's official response to The Queen Mother's speech was to be his last duty before retirement – an occasion regarded by everyone con-

A word with some of the 800 St John Ambulance members packed into Hatfield Polytechnic Hall at the last minute because of heavy rain. Escorting The Queen Mother are Area Commissioner William Appleton (left) and Nigel Longmore, who succeeded Mr L.R.N. Percey as County Commissioner.

out to be one of those days that neither the brigade nor their Commandant-in-Chief would forget for a long time.

The royal review was due to be held in the grounds of the old Hatfield Polytechnic, now part of the University of Hertfordshire, and was regarded as something of a personal triumph for Mr Leonard Percey

cerned as a fitting climax to his years of distinguished service with the Order.

Unhappily, just 24 hours before the visit, Mr Percey was rushed to the Queen Elizabeth II hospital at Welwyn Garden City having suffered a heart attack at his home in Welwyn village. This sudden misfortune added considerably to the prob-

*Showing no sign of his
illness Mr Percey
introduces the novelist
Barbara Cartland (a
County Vice-President) to
Queen Elizabeth.*

lems of the organisers, whose programme had already been thrown out of gear by the weather. Continuous heavy rain had forced them to move the entire ceremony – involving more than 800 Brigade members – into the more restricted area of the college's assembly hall.

However, those urgently replanning the schedule hadn't taken into account the determination of their retiring County Commissioner not to miss this important day in his life at any price. On the morning of the visit – after some energetic lobbying by their patient – no fewer than six doctors examined Mr Percey. They then conferred and agreed to let him go to the ceremony on condition that one of them was with him all the time and that he returned to hospital immediately afterwards.

And so it was that, wearing his uniform and full regalia of a Knight of the Order of St John, Mr Percey was driven with his doctor to Hatfield Polytechnic where the two sat quietly in an ante-room until shortly before The Queen Mother's arrival. The arrival itself then provided a somewhat confusing diversion. The royal chauffeur missed the entrance to the college and drove straight on. Members of St Albans City Band – already in the middle of a carefully timed fanfare – continued playing in bewilderment as The Queen Mother sailed by and disappeared up the street. Fortunately the chauffeur quickly spotted his mistake, performed a swift U-turn and managed to reach the entrance before the fanfare had run out.

A few moments later when a beaming Mr Percey appeared to introduce Her Majesty to his fellow Brigade officers, few would have guessed that anything was wrong. As the *Herts Advertiser* reported: 'The Commissioner confounded everyone by carrying out his official duties with aplomb and delivering a speech that betrayed no hint of his serious indisposition.'

No mention was made of his illness when The Queen Mother paid tribute to Mr Percey's long association with the St John Ambulance Brigade and reminded everyone of the debt they owed him for his 17 years of dedicated work as County Commissioner. She had, of course, been aware of the situation from the outset, not least because Sir Martin Gilliat also lived in Welwyn and had known Mr Percey for a long time. The whole occasion was an unqualified success and Mr Percey returned to hospital where he completed his recovery.

Some years later, however, Queen Elizabeth revealed another reason why she, too, would never forget the day. When a senior Brigade officer met her at another function and recalled the Hatfield inspection, The Queen Mother told him that it was the only occasion at which she had had to carry three versions of the same speech in her handbag. The ever-resourceful Sir Martin, catering for all eventualities, had prepared one speech to be read if Mr Percey was there, a second to be read if he was still in hospital and the third to be read if he had died!

Also in the line-up was Sir Martin Gilliat, carefully maintaining a discreet silence about the elaborate preparations he had made for The Queen Mother's speech that day.

1969

A chat with a master craftsman

When the telephone in Ashwell Rectory rang late one Saturday evening in July 1969 the Reverend Jack Catterick couldn't have guessed that he was about to be given little more than 12 hours' notice to organise a royal visit. The caller was Lady Bowes Lyon, who was entertaining The Queen Mother during her summer stay at the Bury and – trying to think of somewhere new to take her that weekend – had suggested over dinner that they might drive to Ashwell to look round the village's magnificent 14th-century church.

This was one of those spontaneous outings that Queen Elizabeth has always relished. Completely informal. No red carpet. No advance publicity and therefore no need for special security. An opportunity to spend a little time getting as close as any queen can to being 'one of the people'. So there would be no need to keep other visitors out of the church, Lady Bowes Lyon

St Mary's church, Ashwell.

said, but they would be very pleased if someone could meet them and show them round.

That was how St Mary's churchwarden Eric Gurney found himself standing at the lych-gate in Mill Street the next day, trying hard to look nonchalant as he exchanged greetings with villagers hurrying home through the drizzle after a lunchtime drink at the Bushel and Strike. Having been sworn to secrecy, Eric informed those who inquired that he was 'just waiting for a visitor'.

He did become a little concerned about a man lurking in the doorway of Crumps butcher's shop – until the stranger came over and introduced himself as The Queen Mother's personal detective. As it turned out, he was the only policeman present that afternoon when the guests arrived, not in the usual Rolls Royce with its motor-cycle outriders and patrol car escort, but in what turned out to be 'a pretty ordinary car' driven by Lady Bowes Lyon.

On the Sunday of the celebrations to mark her 80th birthday, The Queen Mother tours the photographic exhibition in All Saints with its memories of years past. Escorting her is the Suffragen Bishop of Hertford.

In 1991 with Hertfordshire's Chief Constable Bill Skitt at the opening of the new Royston police station. It was also the 150th anniversary of the county force, which explains the old-fashioned uniforms worn by Her Majesty's guard of honour.

(opposite) Watching the carnival procession from the Bury terrace in 1990 with her nephew Simon Bowes Lyon, as the celebrations for The Queen Mother's 90th birthday begin.

(below) A rare photograph showing The Queen Mother wearing spectacles in public, at the centenary of the Diocese of St Albans in 1977, with the Rt Rev Lord Runcie, then Bishop of St Albans, and the Mayor, Councillor John Dymoke. In later years she has preferred to work from notes printed in large type.

A shy man, Percy Sheldrick (see next page) preferred not to come out to be photographed when The Queen Mother left after her visit. Also in the picture are the rector, Jack Catterick, and his churchwarden Eric Gurney.

As the rector began his improvised tour of St Mary's, it became clear that the other visitors were going to have something more than church history to talk about that evening. None more so than three Stevenage schoolgirls – Rosemary Lovett, Kim Gash and Denise Horler – who found themselves involved in a lengthy discussion with The Queen Mother on the unlikely topic of the Black Death. Working on a thesis about the devastation of Europe's population by the bubonic plague in the 14th century, they had come to Ashwell to make copies of the famous medieval graffiti on a wall inside the church tower.

The Latin inscription is believed to have been scratched into the clunch stone by a builder after some of his workmen and villagers had fallen to the plague. Roughly translated, it reads: '*Miserable, wild, distracted. The dregs of the people alone survive to witness. 1350.*' Other writing refers to a violent storm that swept the country on St Maurice's Day (15th January) eleven years later, causing great damage to local buildings: '*And in the end a tempest, full mighty this year 1361, St. Maur, thunders the world.*'

Clearly fascinated by the inscriptions, Queen Elizabeth asked the girls if she could see the work they had been doing. They dutifully handed over their sketch books which she studied for several minutes before returning them with a smile and the comment: 'Well done! That's very good work.'

One of the most eye-catching features of St Mary's is the tapestry work of Percy Sheldrick, who was verger there for many years. A quite remarkable craftsman, his banners and altar pieces decorate many parts of the church. Perhaps the most outstanding is to be found in the Lady Chapel, where a beautiful reredos made almost entirely of gold thread adorns the tiny altar as a memorial to his mother.

Verger Percy Sheldrick displays a tapestry cushion he made for St Paul's Cathedral.

When Queen Elizabeth saw Percy's work and was told that he lived in the village, she immediately asked to meet him. This unexpected request sent Eric Gurney hot-foot round to Percy's little bungalow in Back Street to inform him that he had just been added to the itinerary of a royal visit about which he had heard nothing. Then approaching his 80th birthday, Percy was doing his washing up at the time and replied with commendable calmness: 'Well, I'm in a bit of a mess, Eric. See if you can hold her back for a few minutes while I tidy things up.'

Percy's request for a delaying tactic presented no problems as it happened because by this time The Queen Mother was heading for Ashwell's tiny museum where she spent 20 minutes examining its display of local artefacts. So all was just about in apple-pie order when Her Majesty – umbrella aloft – was shown along Percy's garden path and into the tiny front room of his council bungalow.

It was there that Queen Elizabeth spent the remainder of her visit, examining more of Percy's work and hearing about his career as a tapestry-weaver. How – as a boy of 10 – he had been taught the basics of embroidery by an old lady living in the village and then, after being badly wounded in France during the Great War, how he had taken up the craft as a full-time career, becoming a master weaver for William Morris, one of the country's leading tapestry manufacturers. 'What a craftsman!' exclaimed his visitor as she emerged to join those who had been waiting outside. 'I have never seen such needlework!'

Then, with Ashwell's rain-swept streets as empty as they were when she arrived, The Queen Mother departed for St Paul's Walden Bury and tea. Most of the village was still unaware that she had been in their midst. As the car disappeared round the corner, those left turned to Percy for his reaction. A shy and gentle man not given to displays of emotion, he allowed himself a smile as he declared the visit to be 'a great honour' and revealed that he had been waiting all week for something unusual to occur. 'You see, the Lord told me earlier this month that something important was going to happen to me,' he said, 'but I must confess I hadn't expected this!'

Percy died in October 1979 in his ninetieth year. His name lives on in his remarkable craftsmanship, which can still be seen on display in Ashwell village church, as well as two other places of worship rather better known to The Queen Mother. For at both St Paul's Cathedral and Westminster Abbey are altar cushions embroidered by Percy Sheldrick to commemorate anniversaries in the history of these great religious buildings.

1970

'To the pioneers of yesterday'

uring their endless round of civic functions, as they cope graciously with the inevitable lines of formal handshakes, royal visitors are always the first to appreciate an imaginative diversion. One that particularly pleased The Queen Mother occurred during the Golden Jubilee celebrations at Welwyn Garden City, when she found herself meeting some of the town's original residents.

After Letchworth (founded in 1903), Welwyn was the second of Britain's new towns to incorporate the garden city ideals of Sir Ebenezer Howard and, like Letchworth, it is still regarded as one of the best. With a spectacular central boule- vard, tree-lined crescents and squares of stylish neo-Georgian houses and a general feeling of light and space, it has become almost essential viewing for architects and town planners from all over the world.

Welwyn's architect, Louis de Soissons, spent 40 years perfecting the town's layout and supervising development. He died in 1962 and eight years later, on his town's 50th anniversary, The Queen Mother came to open the Louis de Soissons Memorial Garden. It is sited on the Campus, the focal point of the town centre where, in 1920, de Soissons and his team began work in one of several old army huts that had been brought in for use as temporary offices.

A bird's eye view of the guard of honour and guests who welcomed The Queen Mother to Welwyn Garden City Campus for the Golden Jubilee celebrations in 1970.

In her tribute to the architect, Queen Elizabeth said Welwyn and Letchworth were the prototypes on which more than 30 new towns had subsequently been based. She reminded everyone of the famous inscription on Sir Christopher Wren's tomb in St Paul's Cathedral and that the same words could be applied to Louis de Soissons: 'You seek my memorial, look around you.'

In the year that de Soissons began work in his wooden hut on the Campus a young couple now acknowledged as the garden city's first residents also moved to the town – even though their home was not

(centre) Touring the Golden Jubilee exhibition, Welwyn's royal visitor cautiously sampled some home-made wine at the stand run by the local Winemakers' Guild.

Molly Jennings, first resident of Welwyn Garden City, receiving her commemorative silver goblet, engraved: 'From the citizens of today to the pioneers of yesterday.'

yet built. Mason and Molly Jennings, then in their early twenties, had chosen a bunga-low plot in High Oak Road. At the time they lived in a gipsy-style caravan at Esher in Surrey and, when told it would be a year before their new home could be com-pleted, they decided to hire a horse to pull their caravan to Hertfordshire and stake their claim. The journey took five days after which, having found a site for their caravan in the rickyard of a friendly farmer, they sent the hired horse back to Esher by rail.

For some months, they lived the kind of spartan existence one tends to associate with the early garden city pioneers – wash-ing with cold water in a tin bath in one of

the barns and cooking meals on a tiny range or over a fire in the rickyard. However, when the weather became bit-terly cold and Mason and Molly woke up to find their pillows stuck to the caravan wall with ice, they gratefully accepted the farmer's invitation to spend the rest of the winter in his house.

All this time Mason was having to don his city clothes each morning to take the train to London where he worked as an accountant. This became an adventure in itself because the garden city then had no station, only a level-crossing halt where passengers had to clamber up into the car-riages. Once on board, they hurriedly changed from mud-spattered gum boots into shoes, throwing the boots out of the carriage window as the train pulled away.

These were then collected by a porter, who sorted them into pairs and placed them in neat rows to await the return of their owners in the evening!

Meanwhile, having trained in architecture at the Royal College of Art, Molly quickly found work as a draughtswoman in Louis de Soisson's drawing office, where

way to the unbuilt city with their horse-drawn caravan. Molly – a widow by this time – was the only woman among 19 pioneer residents the organisers had been able to trace to meet the royal visitor. Among the others were Jack Barnes, a fireman; Charlie Archer, a builder; Sid Bunnage, a council workman and Fred Hopkins who used to

she remained for several years, helping with the design of the garden city. The couple quickly integrated with the growing community and were involved in founding many of the arts, music and drama groups that are such a strong feature of Welwyn's social life today.

At the Golden Jubilee exhibition in 1970, Queen Elizabeth saw a famous local photograph taken 50 years earlier and showing Mason and Molly Jennings on their

cycle from St Albans each day to instal the plumbing in the new homes.

'What a lovely idea!' said Queen Elizabeth as she chatted her way along the line-up, listening to the veterans' stories and then presenting them with their memento of the big day – for the men a silver tankard and for Molly a wine goblet. On each was engraved their name and the inscription: 'From the citizens of today to the pioneers of yesterday.'

Having hired a sturdy carthorse to tow them to their new life in Hertfordshire, Mason and Molly Jennings were photographed on their caravan as they approached the site of the new city in 1920.

1980-1997

The celebration years

'Every day is a new adventure'

'Royalty puts a human face on the operations of Government; and The Queen Mother helps us to feel that being a citizen of this country is not just being an entry on a central computer, but is being a member of a family . . . she has shown a human face which has called out affection and loyalty and the sense of belonging, without which a nation loses its heart.'

It was a former Bishop of St Albans, Robert Runcie, who found the words that seemed to describe exactly her role in the nation's life. Then newly-appointed as Archbishop of Canterbury, Lord Runcie was speaking during the Service of Thanksgiving at St Paul's Cathedral when 2,700 people joined The Queen Mother and her family in celebration of her 80th birthday.

That same month of July in 1980, Her Majesty's other beloved St Paul's (The Walden) did her proud as well, with birthday celebrations lasting several weeks. These had already begun when Queen Elizabeth arrived at the Bury for her customary weekend, the highlight of which was a procession of carnival floats. She watched from the terrace of the big house before setting off on foot across the hayfield to chat to some of the dozens of villagers who had dressed up their floats and themselves in a variety of colourful birthday themes.

On the Sunday, regular worshippers at All Saints joined Queen Elizabeth for Parish Eucharist in the 12th-century church of her baptism. The surprise awaiting her there was a display of enlarged photographs depicting family life and memorable events during the eight decades of her life.

The parish's ambitious programme of celebrations, which included a flower festival in the church, a lakeside concert and firework display, raised more than £3,000 for local charities. In a letter of thanks to the Chairman of the Celebrations Committee, Christopher Mann, Simon Bowes Lyon suggested (in hope more than certainty, no doubt) 'Let us do it again when she is 90!'

Which is how Mr Mann found himself organising a similar successful programme ten years later. 'Happy and Glorious', the popular display of royal photographs was updated and placed once more in the church and another carnival of decorated floats paraded through Whitwell village and up the hill to the big house, where Queen Elizabeth watched from the terrace as she had done in 1980.

These enjoyable family weekends must have reminded The Queen Mother of years before when she was the little-known, youngest daughter of the Bowes Lyon clan. Vivacious, with a taste for strawberries, chocolate cake and black satin dresses; helping out at village fetes, organising picnics for the children and playing energetic games of rounders on the Bury lawns.

There must have been moments, recalling old times with tenants and estate

A pause on the garden seat presented by St Paul's Walden parishioners. Queen Elizabeth is looking through a birthday scrapbook just presented by local schoolchildren.

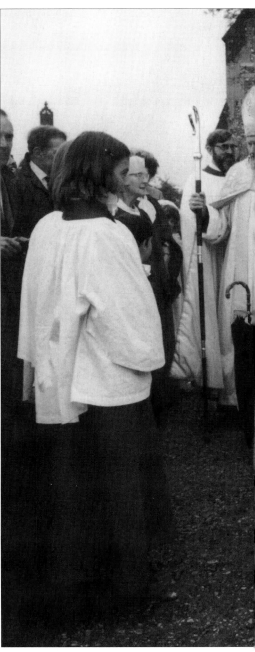

was in darkness. Next morning, he was back at work sorting out his greenhouse when Queen Elizabeth popped her head round the door. 'Ah, Colin,' she said. 'I thought you'd like to know that it's a good many years since I have been serenaded under my window like that.' Which left the Bury's nightingale worrying over which particular bar-room ballad he had been singing as he passed beneath the window of the royal apartment!

Watching the carnival procession from the Bury terrace in 1980 with Lady Bowes Lyon and her son Simon, as the celebrations for The Queen Mother's 80th birthday begin.

workers she had known for years, when it seemed she had never been away. On her 80th birthday, there was Bert King, the retired head gamekeeper who used to accompany The King on his shoots and with whom she had a ritual whenever she passed his cottage on summer walks. 'How are the cherries this year?' she would ask. On which cue, Bert would invite her into his little orchard to pick herself a handful to sample.

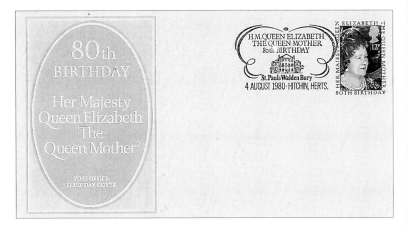

A Post Office first day cover for the 80th birthday celebrations was issued at Hitchin, bearing a special St Paul's Walden franking.

A former head gardener, Colin Byatt, told a story against himself about The Queen Mother's mischievous sense of humour. As a man who greatly enjoyed a drink and a sing-song in the Strathmore Arms on Friday evenings, Colin was still in fine voice as he wended his way home late one night. On a sudden impulse he decided to take a short cut across the lawns in front of the big house, which by then

Having announced on her 80th birthday that she had no intention of retiring, The Queen Mother has kept up a busy programme throughout her 'celebration years'. It was during this period, in 1986, that a family tradition was revived when her nephew Simon Bowes Lyon was appointed Lord Lieutenant of Hertfordshire – assuming the post once held by his father. That same summer Queen Elizabeth was at the Bury again, for the Golden Jubilee celebrations of the Hertfordshire Conservation Society of which she has been a keen supporter from its early days.

Since her 90th birthday, there have been two big 'Queen Mum' engagements in the county. For the first, marking the 150th anniversary of the county police force in 1991, she made a helicopter trip to Royston to open the town's new police station. Then, in May 1993, she returned once more to St Albans Abbey for the Evensong

Meeting the choir and parishioners after the service.

(over the page) Walking to All Saints' church with the Rev Dendle French in July 1990. Now chaplain to the Bowes Lyon family estate at Glamis, Mr French returned to his old parish for The Queen Mother's 90th birthday celebrations. The Right Rev Lord Runcie recalls that 'Dendle is a great favourite with Queen Elizabeth and when I was at Canterbury she would report to me that he was doing well and in no circumstances was he to be moved!'

A word with the latest generation of St Albans' citizens during Queen Elizabeth's last (to date) major official engagement in Hertfordshire, the re-hallowing of the shrine at St Albans Abbey in 1993. With her are Bishop John Taylor and her nephew Simon Bowes Lyon, Lord Lieutenant of the County – as was his father, Sir David, when she came to accept the Freedom of the City more than 30 years earlier.

(below) Lady Bowes Lyon with the Queen Mother's nephew, the Earl of Lichfield, who opened the exhibition of photographs in All Saint's Church.

service at which the restored Shrine of St Alban was rehallowed.

However, if the official engagements are now fewer, Queen Elizabeth's private visits to the county have continued: to Simon and Caroline Bowes Lyon at St Paul's Walden – where she has joined family and parishioners for Holy Communion at All Saints – and to the Salisburys at Hatfield House.

It was at Hatfield one Tuesday in July 1996 that Hertfordshire's indefatigable Queen made an unexpected public appearance during a private party with Lord and Lady Salisbury. His lordship, like his guest, had recently acquired a battery-powered golf buggy to take him about the

The Chairman of Kodak, Mr Erroll Yates, (right) presents Queen Elizabeth with a reproduction of the painting by Alexandra Calani Chile depicting the Earl and Countess of Strathmore and their family at Glamis in Edwardian times, 1990.

(opposite) The font at All Saints, where the baby Elizabeth Bowes Lyon was christened, decorated for the celebrations.

grounds, and was keen to show it off. As a result, visitors quietly admiring the flower displays in the historic West Gardens found themselves having to scatter when the buggy suddenly appeared with Lord Salisbury at the wheel, The Queen Mother by his side and Lady Salisbury perched side-saddle on the back. The crowd watched with a mixture of disbelief and delight as the machine whizzed past them on its journey round the flower beds, with two slightly breathless security men in its wake and the remaining luncheon guests, including the French Ambassador and the Bishop of St Albans, trying none too successfully to keep up!

At this point in Her Majesty's life it is tempting to ask the rather inconsequential question: 'What if Elizabeth Bowes Lyon

had not won the heart of a young man destined to become a King and Emperor and had continued to live among us here in Hertfordshire instead?'

Well, one possibility is that she could have found herself doing a Saturday shift on a stall at Hitchin Market, helping Lady Bowes Lyon weigh out fruit and vegetables from the St Paul's Walden Bury kitchen gardens. Had that been the case there's no doubt that she would have enjoyed it enormously. For – as was well illustrated by that golf buggy jaunt at the age of nearly 96 – Queen Elizabeth's attitude to life remains exactly as it was described long ago by her good friend and equerry, Sir Martin Gilliat:

'Nothing can ever be dull with The Queen Mother. Every day is a new adventure.'

Acknowledgements

The author is grateful to the following for their kind help during his research for this book:

The late Lady (Rachel) Bowes Lyon; The Lord Lieutenant of Hertfordshire, Mr Simon Bowes Lyon; Philip Birtles, Chairman of the de Havilland Aircraft Museum Trust; Beryl Carrington M.B.E. of the *Herts Advertiser*, St Albans; Group Captain John Cunningham; the Revd Dendle French; Lt-Col. K J Grapes of the Royal National Rose Society; Robin Harcourt Williams M.A., F.S.A., Librarian and Archivist to The Marquess of Salisbury; Peter Harkness; Christopher Mann; the Rt Revd Lord Runcie; Lt-Col J D Sainsbury O.B.E., T.D., F.S.A.; Ruth Tarling; the Rev W F Upchurch; Mr W F Wright of Bishops Stortford Museum.

Also to Home Counties Newspapers, plc, for access to their newspaper archives at St Albans and Hitchin; to Stephen Austin Newspapers Ltd (*The Hertfordshire Mercury*) and to the *Herts & Essex Observer*.

I am also grateful to the following for permission to reproduce photographs:

MARJORIE ASHURST *pp.* 17 & 42; GINA BIGGS *p.* 56; BISHOP'S STORTFORD COLLEGE *pp.* 50–51; BRYAN BISHOP *p.* 50 left; STUDIO NEILL, BIGGLESWADE Front cover, *pp.* 2, 77, 79, 86, 87, 88 top, 89, 90, 91 bottom and 93; BERYL CARRINGTON *pp.* 39, 61–63; NEVILLE CHUCK, MID-ANGLIA NEWSPAPERS *p.* 78 top; THE COMMISSION FOR THE NEW TOWNS AND KEN WRIGHT *pp.* 83 & 84 left; DE HAVILLAND AIRCRAFT MUSEUM TRUST *pp.* 48, 49 & 59 top; EAST HERTS NHS TRUST *p.* 29; FIRST GARDEN CITY HERITAGE MUSEUM *pp.* 36 & 44; PETER JOHN GATES *p.* 76; DEREK GEORGE *p.* 60; ANTHONY V GREGORY *pp.* 61, 70–71, 73–75, 78 bottom, 83–84 centre; HARKNESS ROSES *pp.* 59 bottom, 68 top; HARRY HAND *pp.* 10 & 67; HERTFORDSHIRE CONSTABULARY *p.* 91 top; HERTFORDSHIRE GUIDES *p.* 30; HERTFORD MUSEUM AND THE *HERTS MERCURY pp.* 45 & 46; HITCHIN MUSEUM *pp.* 7, 13, 38 and 54; ALAN JAMES *p.* 53 bottom; KODAK LTD *p.* 92; ALAN MILLARD *HITCHIN COMET pp.* 34–35 & 80; NORTH HERTS NHS TRUST *pp.* 28; DIANA POHLMANN *p.* 81; THE PRIORY SCHOOL, HITCHIN *pp.* 8–9, 53 top and 66; ROYAL CALEDONIAN SCHOOLS EDUCATIONAL TRUST *p.* 52; ROYAL NATIONAL ROSE SOCIETY *p.* 68 bottom; THE MARQUESS OF SALISBURY *p.* 43; BILL SMITH *p.* 82; WELWYN GARDEN CITY REFERENCE LIBRARY *p.* 85 right

Other photographs are from the author's collection.

Index